D0916507

Adventures
in the
Unknown
Interior
of
America

Cabeza de Vaca's

Adventures
in the
Unknown
Interior
of
America

Translated and Edited by Cyclone Covey
with an Epilogue by William T. Pilkington

UNIVERSITY OF NEW MEXICO PRESS

ALBUQUERQUE

Cordially dedicated to
Vernon A. Chamberlin

Preface

THIS SIXTEENTH-CENTURY odyssey of Cabeza de Vaca's
is one of the great true epics of history. It is the semi-
official report to the king of Spain by the ranking surviving
officer of a royal expedition to conquer Florida which fan-
tastically miscarried.

Four out of a land-force of 300 men—by wits, stamina
and luck—found their way back to civilization after eight
harrowing years and roughly 6,000 miles over mostly
unknown reaches of North America. They were the first
Europeans to see and live to report the interior of Florida,
Texas, New Mexico, Arizona and northernmost Mexico;
the 'possum and the buffalo; the Mississippi and the
Pecos; pine-nut mash and mesquite-bean flour; and a long
string of Indian Stone Age tribes. What these wanderers
merely heard and surmised had just as great an effect on
subsequent events as what they learned at first hand.

Their sojourn "to the sunset," as they told certain of the
Indians in the latters' idiom, took on a great added interest and value in the 1930's with the convergent discovery of Carl Sauer and Cleve Hallenbeck that Cabeza
de Vaca and his companions had traveled, for the most
part, over Indian trails that were still traceable. The
thorough work of these two distinguished professors, plus
that of innumerable others in such disciplines as archae-
ology, anthropology, cartography, geology, climatology,
botany, zoology and history, has given surprisingly sharp
definition to much of the old narrative that had hitherto
seemed vague and baffling. The present translation is the

first to take advantage of the scientific findings of half a century which culminate in Sauer and Hallenbeck. Hallenbeck, in fact, incorporates and supersedes all previous scholarship on the subject (*Álvar Núñez Cabeza de Vaca: The Journey and Route of the First European to Cross the Continent of North America:* Glendale, Calif.: Arthur H. Clark, 1940).

It was Álvar Núñez's mother, Doña Teresa, whose surname was Cabeza de Vaca, or Head of a Cow. This name originated as a title of honor from the decisive Battle of Las Navas de Tolosa in the Sierra Morenas on 12 July 1212, when a peasant named Alhaja detected an unguarded pass and marked it with a cow's skull. A surprise attack over this pass routed the Moorish enemy. King Sancho of Navarre thereupon created the novel title, Head of a Cow, and bestowed it in gratitude upon the peasant Alhaja. Álvar Núñez proudly adopted this surname of his mother's, though that of his father, de Vera, had a lustre from recent imperialism. Pedro de Vera, the sadistic conqueror of the Canaries, was Álvar Núñez's grandfather. Álvar Núñez, the eldest of his parents' four children, spoke proudly of his paternal grandfather. It may have been significant for the boy's later career in America that he listened to old Pedro repeat his tales of heroism, and that he had a childhood familiarity with the conquered Guanche savages with whom the grandfather staffed his household as slaves.

Álvar Núñez Cabeza de Vaca, who was born about 1490, grew up in the little Andalusian wine center of Jérez, just a few miles from Cádiz and fewer still from the port San Lúcar de Barrameda at the mouth of the Guadalquivir. This is the port Magellan sailed from in September 1519—and Cabeza de Vaca, seven years and ten months later. Cabeza de Vaca was about ten years old when Columbus, aged forty-nine, returned to Cádiz in chains. The boy may well have seen the autocratic admiral thus —just as he himself was to be returned to the same city in chains at the age of fifty-three.

In the tradition of the landed gentry, Cabeza de Vaca turned to a military career while still in his teens. When about twenty-one, he marched in the army which King Ferdinand sent to aid Pope Julius II in 1511, and saw action in the Battle of Ravenna of 11 April 1512 in which 20,000 died. He served as ensign at Gaeta outside Naples before returning to Spain and to the service of the Duke of Medina Sidonia in 1513 in Seville, the metropolis of his home region. In the Duke's service, Cabeza de Vaca survived the Comuneros civil war (including the recapture of the Alcázar, 16 September 1520, from the Sevillian rebels), the battles of Tordesillas and Villalar, and finally, warfare against the French in Navarre.

He was a veteran of sufficient distinction by 1527 to receive the royal appointment of second in command in the Narváez expedition for the conquest of Florida, a territory which at that time was conceived as extending indefinitely westward. This appointment saved him from another Italian campaign; Charles V's Spanish and German troops ingloriously sacked Rome itself barely a month before the Narváez expedition sailed. Cabeza de Vaca married, apparently, only a short time before the sailing, though there is a bare possibility that he postponed marriage to his return.

The red-bearded, one-eyed chief commander, or governor, Pámfilo de Narváez, was a grasping bungler. He lost an eye when he took an expedition from Cuba to Mexico in jealousy to arrest Cortés. Cortés first won over most of his 900 troops and then roundly defeated the rest. Narváez was arrested wounded. As governor of Cuba, he had calmly sat on a horse one day and watched his men massacre 2,500 Indians who were distributing food to the Spaniards. It was his stupid decision to separate his cavalry and infantry from their sustaining ships that sealed the doom of his expedition in Florida—as Cabeza de Vaca forewarned in vain.

One of the interesting undercurrents of Cabeza de Vaca's narrative, which refrains from critical remarks about the Governor, is the implicit antagonism between

them. Narváez deliberately sent Cabeza de Vaca on dirty-
work reconnaissances, sent him into a possibly hostile village first, put him in charge of the more dangerous van-
guard while he brought up the rear, and tried to get rid
of him by assigning him to the ships. The climax of their
rivalry came when Cabeza de Vaca dramatized his cor-
rectness in asking·the Governor for orders while the Governor was running out on the majority of his expeditionaries.

The modern reader may at first find himself carried
along by his interest in the expeditionaries' struggle for
survival, but in time will likely grow increasingly interested
in the struggle for survival of the aborigines. Cabeza de
Vaca's ability to survive depended in large measure on his
capacity to adjust to them and identify with them. His
induplicable anthropological information on the paleolithic
and neolithic cultures of coast, forest, river, plains, mountain, and desert tribes presents hitherto untapped "news
of the human race" on a considerable scale. Anthropologists and psychologists can make much of such data as, for
instance, the prevalence of illnesses due to hysteria. The
reactions of the retreating expeditionaries to a variety of
extreme tests constitute an important section of the "news
of the human race" in this little book. One, of their first
tests, though not so mortal a one, was the blandishments
of Santo Domingo. Another of the preliminary tests—a
kind of harbinger of the tragedies to come—was the hurricane that caught the expedition in Cuba. And among the
many firsts of Cabeza de Vaca's narrative, this is the first
description in literature·of a West Indies hurricane.

Cabeza de Vaca gives an unvarnished, soldierly account
of what he went through in the years 1527-37 which leaves
much to be inferred—and much is inferrable. He passes
up most of his opportunities to dwell on morbidity or his
own heroism, fiercely jealous though he is of his honor
and tantalizing as is the possibility, to him, of his having
received divine favor. He remains the central figure and
guiding spirit throughout the epic, even if omitting to
mention this role most of the time. It was his resilience

and resourcefulness and, above all, venturousness which gave momentum to the survivors' sojourn. The others who got back with him had, in one stretch of years, come to a paralyzed impasse which could not be broken until he joined them. He had been actively working himself out of servitude as a far-wandering merchant during these same years. He would attempt cures and operations that others would quail from. Even toward the end, at the climax, he could not induce his fellow Spaniards to rush on ahead, but went himself.

He must have had a penchant for austerity. In time, all four survivors were thriving on it—walking all day and eating only one meal, a spare one at evening, and feeling no weariness. Even the Indians were amazed. One suspects that his companions had less zest for this life and harbored some resentment at being thus driven. They had twice given him up for dead and gone on without verification.

The Indians found Castillo the most attractive most of the time; and it becomes an interesting puzzle to try to ascertain why, from the limited evidence given. Captain Castillo was a well-bred *hidalgo* from the university town of Salamanca, the son of a distinguished and learned father. He was the least bold of the four survivors and the one who slipped most quickly and quietly into obscurity when the trek was over. He is the one who taught the other four the art of faith-healing; yet he felt the most inhibitions in exercising the art because of a sense of unworthiness. Maybe Castillo was really the one responsible for deepening Cabeza de Vaca's mechanical religiousness to genuine devoutness. Cabeza de Vaca, in any event, learned a lot. Both Castillo and Dorantes, we see early in the narrative in Florida, had a certain rapport with Cabeza de Vaca; and Dorantes intended to continue in association with him after the journey's end in Mexico City.

The Pimas in northern Sonora presented Dorantes with the more than 600 opened deer hearts, and desert Indians in New Mexico had given him a precious copper rattle. He seems gradually to have displaced Castillo as the Indian favorite; but it is Cabeza de Vaca who emerges clearly dominant at the last.

When he returned to Spain in 1537, ten hard years older and wiser, his consuming ambition was to go back to the region in which he had so frequently faced death, as first in command. A half-year's delay in getting home to Spain, occasioned by the capsizing of his intended ship at Veracruz, may have been the factor which gave the leadership to De Soto instead. De Soto did all he could to engage Cabeza de Vaca as his second in command, but after Cabeza de Vaca's experience under the incompetent Narváez, he could not consent to seconding any commander again. One reason he wished to go back to "Florida" was his belief in the land's possibilities for agriculture, grazing, and mining—especially for gold, silver, emeralds, and turquoises. He also had become convinced that a fabulous aboriginal nation existed in the north, not far beyond the perimeter of his recent circuit, and another on the Pacific, which he believed much nearer the northern pueblos than was remotely possible. The evidence he gives of these opulent places quickly convinced many others. They, in fact, leaped to connect the unseen pueblos across the desert with the legendary Seven Cities of Cíbola, which supposedly had been founded somewhere in the west in the eighth century by seven fugitive bishops.

The evidence he withheld was equally convincing. Not forgetting that he had gone out on a military expedition responsible to the Crown, he felt he should not divulge much of his new knowledge before he had first reported to the king. He also did not wish anyone else to get the jump on him in picking the "Florida" plum; so he hated to divulge what might entice others to apply to the king or what would help ensure their success. He and Dorantes hoped to return to the north together. Their very reticence fired imaginations and greed and became in itself a kind of proof of marvels. The fact that Cabeza de Vaca inadvertently left his six "emerald" arrowheads behind on the Sinaloa and could not produce the mere malachite specimens for examination gave his guarded testimony about emeralds and other precious minerals uncontradictable authority. He, of course, believed them genuine; the turquoises he had been given actually were.

When Cabeza de Vaca sincerely represented the possible riches of the unexplored country to the north in glowing terms to the viceroy (for the viceroy was the personal representative of the king), Mendoza promptly set about acting on the intelligence. Both the Fray Marcos and Coronado expeditions materialized from the direct stimulus of Cabeza de Vaca's return and reports. He repeated his confidence in the new region to Charles V in person, as well as in his full, printed report which he shared with the public in October 1542. (The viceroy had earlier transmitted a report to the king which has not survived.) At the time of De Soto's preparations, when Cabeza de Vaca's hopes of leading a Florida expedition had long since collapsed, he still kept his pact with Dorantes and would not even brief his kinsmen who had accepted commands with De Soto. But he did confidentially advise them by all means to sell their estates and go. In the long run, he far underestimated the potential of this new region, but a terrible disillusionment with it inevitably set in after a few more expeditions went through the sort of suffering the Narváez "conquerors" had experienced.

There was a more compelling reason than riches for Cabeza de Vaca's sanguine view: He had learned to love the land as beautiful and the Indians as surpassingly handsome, strong, and intelligent. In the midst of his sufferings, he caught a vision of the brotherhood of man. He wanted to bring the Indians civilization and Christianity and to establish a humane order among them. He had found that he could cure their sicknesses, communicate Christian teachings, and compose their tribal hostilities, leaving the lands he passed through in peace. The immediate result of his return—still 900 miles before he reached Mexico City—was to stop the slave raids in Sonora and Sinaloa and induce the terrified refugee population to return and rebuild their villages and cultivate the soil once more. In his strongest language, he urged an unrapacious, peaceful winning of the Indians to king and Christ. He went so far as to say that this was the only sure way to "conquer" them. The great irony of his impressive demonstration is the scale of the brutality with which the lesson was violated.

His devotion to the dual and somewhat contradictory codes of the knight and the Christian gentleman made Cabeza de Vaca appear at times quixotic to his contemporaries (nearly a century before the dear old Don); yet it was the crass, "practical" men who failed and who contributed to the failure of many others. Cabeza de Vaca succeeded, and saved three others. He would have saved many more—possibly the entire expedition—had more of the men matched his own valor and responsibleness, particularly the chief commander, Narváez, who at the last thought only of his own survival, and did not survive.

Since De Soto had already received the royal commission for Florida (by the time Cabeza de Vaca got back to Spain), the king came through with the alternative appointment of *adelantado* (governor) of the considerable South American provinces of the Río de la Plata, to which Cabeza de Vaca sailed in 1540.

His first concern on assuming office was to rescue the Indian-beleaguered and disease-wasting colony of Asunción. Instead of the year-long sea route via Buenos Aires, he chose to lead an expedition directly overland—1000 miles across unknown and supposedly impenetrable jungles, mountains, and cannibal villages. He accomplished this successfully, barefoot, from late November 1541 to late March 1542, from Santa Catalina Island via Iguazú Falls. The following summer he led an even more remarkable expedition about the same distance up the Paraguay in search of the legendary Golden City of Manoa. Extreme privation, particularly during the tropical rains of the fall, forced him to turn back when his men would go no further. Back at Asunción, he fell victim to intrigue and fever. He had systematically prohibited enslaving, raping, and looting of the Indians—which were what the majority of the Spaniards had come for. So they deposed him. It is a more complicated story than that, however. The soldiers resented his dealing gently and as a divine agent. (He required them to transport a fine camp bed for himself through the jungles.) They returned him wretchedly to Spain in chains in 1543.

Not until 1551 did the Council for the Indies get round to trying him, and then they gave credence to the unscrupulous lieutenant governor who had led the mutiny in La Plata, and sentenced Cabeza de Vaca to banishment to Africa for eight years. His wife loyally spent all her fortune in his behalf and, finally, the king awoke from his habitual stupor, annulled the sentence, awarded Cabeza de Vaca a pension, and placed him on the Audiencia. He died in honor in 1557. His account of his South American adventures, which is three times longer than that of his North American journey, was bound with the second edition of the latter in 1555 under the title *Comentarios.*

Note on the Text

The title of the North American narrative was *La Relación* (The Relation). The second edition had a running title, *Naufragios* (Shipwrecks), which is misleading. There are minor differences in the two editions, and they are noted in the following translation wherever important. The 1542 edition, published at Zamora, has no chapter titles, only periodic breaks in the text. An editor added titles for the 1555 edition, published at Valladolid. They are sometimes inconsistent in style and often miss the crux of the short chapters' content. The chapter divisions, furthermore, sometimes ignore the natural breaks in the narrative. In the following translation, the chapter divisions and titles have occasionally been altered to fit the text better. The paragraphing is also the translator's, on the same principle. (Sixteenth-century books paragraphed infrequently.)

Several passages have been transposed from their original out-of-place locations in the text; all of these transpositions are identified, and the reason for them should appear plain. Interpolated material is given in brackets, which are used in lieu of footnotes to speed and simplify the reading. Clarifying information is kept at a minimum to maintain the continuous flow of the narrative.

Besides the original 1542 edition and the original 1555 edition of the *Relación*, there is also the valuable, and earlier, supplement known as the *Joint Report*. It is a thirty-page summary of the sojourn drawn up by Cabeza de Vaca, Castillo, and Dorantes in Mexico City in 1536 and delivered to the Audiencia·at Santo Domingo by Cabeza de Vaca on his homeward voyage. Its difference in style from the *Relación* suggests Castillo as the penman for his superior education. The original of this document is not known to be in existence. The earliest known version of it—from a 1539 copy—appears in volume III, book 35, of Captain Gonzalo Fernández de Oviedo y Valdés: *Historia General y Natural de las Indias, Islas y Tierra-Firme del Mar Océano*, edited by D. José Amador de los Ríos (Madrid 1853). All three of these primary sources have been collated in the following translation.

The *Relación* was translated into Italian in 1556, and this Italian version was the source of the first English version, a paraphrase which appeared in *Purchas His Pilgrimes* in 1613. Spanish reprints came out in 1736, 1749, 1852, and 1906, not counting an 1870 abridgement. A French translation appeared in 1837. Only two full translations have appeared in English: that of Buckingham Smith in 1851 (a revision of which was published posthumously, having been edited by John Gilmary Shea in 1871, and reprinted in Scribner's *Original Narratives of Early American History* series in 1907, edited by Frederick W. Hodge of the Bureau of American Ethnology), and the 1904 translation of Fanny Bandelier, published in 1905, edited by Adolph Bandelier. The translation that follows has been checked against both of these and is deeply indebted to the more literal Smith version. Translated and paraphrased portions of the *Relación* by Sauer and Hellenbeck; the text in the *Biblioteca de Autores Españoles*, XXII (1946); and the abridged Spanish text of José E. Espinosa and E. A. Mercado of 1941, also have proved useful. Morris Bishop, *The Odyssey of Cabeza de Vaca* (Century, 1933), documents the explorer's early life.

Cabeza de Vaca's dates are Old Style. To correlate them to our present calendar, add ten days. The change of New Year's from March 25 to January 1 has, however, already been made in the translation.

Cabeza de Vaca's *league* seems to be the 3.1-mile Spanish league of his time rather than the 2.6-mile, though he may use the latter occasionally. Even his sea distances seem to be in terms of the 3.1-mile league instead of the longer nautical league. In any case, the distances are estimates. They are often amazingly accurate, but starvation, deathly weariness, and oppressive fright more often interfered with mensural judgment. The estimates therefore usually err on the side of exaggeration, though by any reckoning at any time the distances traversed are vast.

The translator-editor herewith acknowledges and thanks the New York Public Library for furnishing him with a microfilm of the 1542 edition of the *Relación* and another of the 1555 edition of the *Relación* and *Comentarios,* and the Library of Congress for a microfilm of the *Joint Report* from Oviedo's *Historia;* also Mary Jaime and Esta Albright of the Interlibrary Loan and Special Services Departments of the Oklahoma State University Library; and Marvin T. Edmison and the OSU Research Foundation; and Richard P. Cecil, the commissioning editor-in-chief.

C. C.

Wake Forest University

Adventures in the Unknown Interior of America-

Adventures in the Unknown Interior of America

Sacred Caesarian Catholic Majesty:

AMONG ALL THE PRINCES who have reigned, I know of none who has enjoyed the universal esteem of Your Majesty [Emperor Charles V] at this day, when strangers vie in approbation with those motivated by religion and loyalty.

Although everyone wants what advantage may be gained from ambition and action, we see everywhere great inequalities of fortune, brought about not by conduct but by accident, and not through anybody's fault but as the will of God. Thus the deeds of one far exceed his expectation, while another can show no higher proof of purpose than his fruitless effort, and even the effort may go unnoticed.

I can say for myself that I undertook the march abroad, on royal authorization, with a firm trust that my service would be as evident and distinguished as my ancestors', and that I would not need to speak to be counted among those Your Majesty honors for diligence and fidelity in affairs of state. But my counsel and constancy availed nothing toward those objectives we set out to gain, in your interests, for our sins. In fact, no other of the many armed expeditions into those parts has found itself in such dire straits as ours, or come to so futile and fatal a conclusion.

My only remaining duty is to transmit what I saw and heard in the nine years I wandered lost and miserable over many remote lands. I hope in some measure to convey to Your Majesty not merely a report of positions and distances, flora and fauna, but of the customs of the numerous, barbarous people I talked with and dwelt among, as well as any other matters I could hear of or observe. My hope of going out from among those nations was always small; nevertheless, I made a point of remembering all the particulars, so that should God our Lord eventually

25

please to bring me where I am now, I might testify to my exertion in the royal behalf.

Since this narrative, in my opinion, is of no trivial value for those who go in your name to subdue those countries and bring them to a knowledge of the true faith and true Lord and bring them under the imperial dominion, I have written very exactly. Novel or, for some persons, difficult to believe though the things narrated may be, I assure you they can be accepted without hesitation as strictly factual. Better than to exaggerate, I have minimized all things; it is enough to say that the relation is offered Your Majesty for truth.

I beg that it may be received as homage, since it is the most one could bring who returned thence naked.

CHAPTER 1:
The Sailing of the Armada

ON 17 JUNE 1527, Governor Pámfilo de Narváez left the port of San Lúcar de Barrameda authorized and commanded by Your Majesty to conquer and govern the provinces which should be encountered from the River of Palms [the Río Grande] to the cape of Florida. His expedition consisted of five ships with about 600 men and the following officers (for they will have to be mentioned): Cabeza de Vaca, Treasurer and *alguacil mayor* [provost marshall]; Alonso Enríquez, Comptroller; Alonso de Solís, Quartermaster to Your Majesty and Inspector; Juan Suárez, a Franciscan friar, Commissary; and four more Franciscan friars.

We arrived at the island of Santo Domingo [about September 17] and there tarried nearly 45 days gathering provisions and particularly horses, during which time the local inhabitants, by promises and proposals, seduced more than 140 of our men to desert.

From that island we sailed to Santiago [de Cuba] where, for some days, the Governor recruited men and further furnished himself with arms and horses. It fell out there that a prominent gentleman, Vasco Porcallo, of Trinidad, a hundred leagues northwest on the same island, offered the Governor some provisions he had stored at home if the Governor could go pick them up. The Governor forthwith headed with the whole fleet to get them, but, on reaching Cabo de Santa Cruz, a port half way, he decided to send Captain [Juan] Pantoja [who had commanded the crossbowmen on Narváez's 1520 expedition to Mexico] to bring the stores back in his ship. For greater security, the Governor sent me along with another ship, while he himself anchored with the remaining four (he had bought an additional ship at Santo Domingo).

27

When we reached the port of Trinidad, Vasco Porcallo conducted Captain Pantoja to the town, a league away, while I stayed at sea with the pilots, who said we ought to get out of there as fast as possible, for it was a very bad port where many vessels had been lost. Since what happened to us there was phenomenal, I think it will not be foreign to the purpose of my narrative to relate it here.

The next morning gave signs of bad weather. Rain started falling and the sea rose so high that I gave the men permission to go ashore; but many of them came back aboard to get out of the wet and cold, unwilling to trek the league into town. A canoe, meanwhile, brought me a letter from a resident of the town requesting me to come for the needed provisions that were there. I excused myself, saying I could not leave the ships. At noon the canoe returned with a more urgent letter, and a horse was brought to the beach for me. I gave the same answer as before, but the pilots and people aboard entreated me to go in order to hasten the provisions as fast as possible; they greatly feared the loss of both ships by further delay in this port.

So I went to the town, first leaving orders with the pilots that should the south wind (which is the one which often wrecks vessels here) whip up dangerously, they should beach the ships at some place where the men and horses could be saved. I wanted to take some of the men with me for company, but they said the weather was too nasty and the town too far off; but tomorrow, which would be Sunday, they intended to come, with God's help, and hear Mass.

An hour after I left, the sea began to rise ominously and the north wind blow so violently that the two boats would not have dared come near land even if the head wind had not already made landing impossible. All hands labored severely under a heavy fall of water that entire day and until dark on Sunday. By then the rain and tempest had stepped up until there was as much agitation in the town as at sea. All the houses and churches went down. We had to walk seven or eight together, locking arms, to keep from being blown away. Walking in the woods gave us as much fear as the tumbling houses, for the trees were falling, too, and could have killed us. We wandered all night in this raging tempest without finding any place we could linger as long as half an hour in safety. Particularly from midnight on, we heard a great roaring and the sound of many voices, of little bells, also flutes, tambourines, and other instruments, most of which lasted till morning, when the storm ceased. Nothing so terrible as this [hurricane] had been seen in these parts before. I drew up an authenticated account of it and sent it back to Your Majesty.

On Monday morning we went down to the harbor but did not find the ships. When we spied the buoys belonging to them floating on the water, we knew the ships had been lost. Hiking along the shore looking for signs of them, we found nothing, so we struck through the marshy woods for about a quarter of a league [about three fourths of a mile] and came upon the little boat of one of the ships lodged in some treetops. Ten leagues farther, along the coast, two bodies were found, belonging to my ship, but they had been so disfigured by beating against the rocks that they could not be recognized. Some lids of boxes, a cloak, and a quilt rent in pieces were also found, but nothing more.

Sixty persons had been lost in the ships, and twenty horses. Those who had gone ashore the day of our arrival —they may have numbered as many as thirty—were all who survived of both ships.

For some days we struggled with much hardship and hunger; for the provisions had been destroyed, also some herds. The country was left in a condition piteous to behold: parched, bereft of grass and leaf, the trees prostrate.

Thus we lived until November 5, when the Governor put in with his four ships, which had run into a safe place in time to live through the great storm. The people who came in them, as well as those on shore, were so unnerved by what had happened that they feared to go on board in the winter. Seconded by the townspeople, they prevailed on the Governor to spend it in Cuba. He put the ships and crews in my charge to take to the port of

Xagua [Jagua, at the entrance to the Bay of Cienfuegos], twelve leagues away, to pass the winter. There I remained until February 20.

CHAPTER 2:
The Governor's Arrival at Xagua with a Pilot

ON THAT DAY the Governor hove in with a brig he had bought in Trindad and, with him, a pilot by the name of Miruelo, who had been hired because he claimed he had been to the River of Palms and knew the whole northern coast. The Governor had also purchased another vessel, which he left beached at Havana with forty people and twelve horsemen under Captain Alvaro de la Cerda.

The second day after the Governor arrived, his expedition set sail—400 men and 80 horses in four ships and a brig. The touted pilot we had taken on ran the vessels aground in the shoals called Canarreo [doubtless one of the keys off the western point of Cuba]; and for fifteen days we stood stranded, the keels often scraping bottom. At last a storm from the south raised the water over the shoals enough to lift us off, though dangerously.

No sooner did we reach Guaniguanico than another tempest nearly finished us and, at Cape Corrientes [southwestern Cuba], we had to battle yet another for three days. Finally passing those places, we doubled Cape Sant Anton [the westernmost tip of Cuba] and made for Havana handicapped by contrary winds.

We got within twelve leagues and next day pointed to enter the harbor when a stout south wind drove us toward Florida.

We sighted land Tuesday, April 12 [1528], and sailed up the [west] coast. On Holy Thursday we came to anchor in the mouth of a bay [perhaps Sarasota Bay], at the head of which we could see some houses and habitations of Indians.

CHAPTER 3:
Our Landing in Florida

THAT SAME DAY [April 14] the comptroller Alonso Enríquez ventured to an island in the bay and called to the Indians, who came and stayed with him quite a while, trading fish and venison for trinkets.

The day following—Good Friday—the Governor debarked with as many men as the ships' little boats could hold. We found the *buhíos* [wigwams of a type which had an open shed attached] deserted, the Indians having fled by canoe in the night. One of the *buhíos* was big enough to accommodate more than 300 people; the others were smaller. Amid some fish nets we found a gold rattle.

Next day the Governor raised flags and took possession of the country in Your Majesty's name, exhibiting his credentials and receiving our acknowledgement of his office, according to Your Majesty's command. We, for our part, laid our commissions before the Governor and he responded appropriately to each. [Narváez, we gather much later, thought of himself as founding a town, La Cruz (The Cross), at this time.]

He then ordered the balance of the men to land, with the horses, of which only 42 had survived the storms and the long passage at sea; these few were too thin and run down to be of much use.

The Indians of the village returned next day and approached us. Because we had no interpreter, we could not make out what they said; but their many signs and threats left little doubt that they were bidding us to go. They, however, went away and interfered no further.

CHAPTER 4:
Our Penetration of the Country

THE DAY FOLLOWING, the Governor resolved to explore inland, taking the Commissary [Fray Suárez], the Inspector [Solís], and me, together with forty men, including six horsemen, who could hardly have done much good.

We headed northward until about the hour of vespers, when we came upon a very big bay which seemed to extend far inland. [This would have been Tampa Bay.] We stayed there overnight, returning the next day to our base camp.

The Governor ordered the brig to coast in search of the harbor which Miruelo, the pilot, had said he knew but which he so far had failed to find; he did not know where we were or where the port was from here. The Governor further ordered that, in case this harbor could not be found, the brig should proceed to Havana, find the ship Alvaro de la Cerda commanded, get them both provisioned, and return together to us.

When the brig had gone, we struck inland again, the same men as before plus others. We followed the shore of the bay we had found and, after four leagues, captured four Indians. We showed them some corn to see whether they knew what it was, for we had so far come across no sign of any. They indicated they would take us where there was some and led us to their village at the head of the bay close by. There they showed us a little corn not yet fit to gather.

We saw a number of crates there like those used for merchandising in Castile, each containing a dead man covered with painted deerskins. The Commissary took this for some form of idolatry and burned the crates and corpses. We also found pieces of linen and woolen cloth

32

and bunches of feathers like those of New Spain. And we saw some nuggets of gold. [The *Joint Report* of Cabeza de Vaca, Castillo, and Dorantes, written in Mexico in 1536 and delivered to the Audiencia at Santo Domingo by Cabeza de Vaca on his homeward voyage in 1537, amplifies that the Governor gave the order for burning the dead bodies and their boxes; that pieces of shoes and canvas and some iron were also found; and that the Indians said by signs that they had found these items in a vessel that had been wrecked in that bay. The *Joint Report* makes it clear that the bodies were Europeans, and blames the friars, not just the Franciscan Commissary, for the burning.]

We inquired of the Indians by signs where these things came from. They gave us to understand that very far from here was a province called Apalachen, where was much gold and plenty of everything we wanted. [The *Joint Report* specifies that it was the gold rather than all the items indiscriminately which came from "Apalache." The Apalachee Indians lived in northwestern Florida, centering on the later Tallahassee and St. Marks. Appalachee Bay and the Appalachian Mountains take their names from this tribe.]

Keeping these Indians for guides, we proceeded another ten or twelve leagues, to a village of fifteen houses, where we saw a large cornfield ready for harvest, some of the ears already dry. After staying two days there, we returned to the base camp and told the Comptroller and pilots what we had seen and what the Indians had told us.

Next day, May 1, the Governor called the Commissary, Comptroller, Inspector, and me, also a sailor named Bartolomé Fernandez and a notary named Jerónimo de Alaniz, and divulged his intention of marching inland while the ships continued to coast on to a port which the pilots asserted lay close to the River of Palms. What, the Governor asked, did we think of this?

It seemed to me, I answered, that under no circumstances should we forsake the ships before they rested in a secure harbor which we controlled; that the pilots, after all, disagreed among themselves on every particular and did not so much as know where we then were; that we would be deprived of our horses in case we needed them; that we could anticipate no satisfactory communication with the Indians, having no interpreter, as we entered an unknown country; and that we did not have supplies to sustain a march we knew not where—no more than a pound of biscuit and a pound of bacon per man being possible from the ships' stores. I concluded that we had better re-embark and look for a harbor and soil better suited to settle, since what we had so far seen was the most desert and poor that had ever been discovered in that region.

Our Commissary [Fray Suárez] took the exact opposite view. He held that we should not embark but should keep to the coast in quest of Pánuco [later renamed Tampico, at the mouth of the Pánuco River on the coast of central Mexico—the northernmost Spanish settlement, founded by Cortés himself in 1522], which the pilots said was only ten or fifteen leagues from here [but which was actually over 600 leagues, i.e., more than 1,800 miles, via the coast]; that we could not miss it, since it extended inland a dozen leagues; that the first to come upon it should wait for the other; that to embark would be to tempt God, after all the adversities we had endured since leaving Spain—so many storms, such losses of men and ships; that we should therefore march along the coast while the ships sailed along it till they joined at the same harbor.

This struck everybody else but the Notary as the best course. The Notary thought the ships should not be left unless in a known, safe, populated harbor; that the Governor might then advance inland at his discretion.

Seeing the Governor was going to overrule my objections, I required him, in the interest of Your Majesty, not to quit the ships before putting them in a secure port, and to certify that I had said such, under the hand of the Notary. The Governor replied that he concurred in the judgment of the Commissary and the other officers and that I had no authority to make these requirements of him. He then bade the Notary, instead, to certify that he was breaking up the settlement he had founded, because the country lacked means of support, and was going in search of the port [Pánuco] and a better land. Thereupon he ordered the mustering and victualing of the men who were to go with him.

Then he turned to me and, in the presence of the whole council, said that since I so opposed and feared marching inland, I should sail in charge of the ships and remaining men, and should establish a settlement in the event I reached the port ahead of him.

I refused.

That same evening, awhile after we had dispersed, he sent word begging me to reconsider, that he could not trust anyone else to command the ships. When I still refused, he wanted to know why. I answered that I felt certain he would never find the ships again, or they him, as anyone could predict from the woefully inadequate preparation; that I would rather hazard the danger that lay ahead in the interior than give any occasion for questioning my honor by remaining safely aboard behind. Seeing he could get nowhere with me himself, he had others reason with and entreat me. But I always gave the same answer.

So he finally named a lieutenant, one Caravallo, to command the ships.

CHAPTER 5:
The Governor's Leave-Taking

ON SATURDAY, May 1—the day of this dispute—the Governor ordered two pounds of buscuit and a half pound of bacon rationed each man who was going with him; and so we took up our march into the interior. Our total force was 300, of whom 40 were horsemen. Those riding horse-back included the Commissary Fray Suárez; another friar, Juan de Palos; three priests; and the frockless officers.

We traveled [northward] for fifteen days on our rations without finding anything edible but palmettos [dwarf fan-palms] like those of Andalusia. In all that time we en-countered not a single person, village, or house. At last we came to a river [the Suwannee], which we swam and rode rafts across with great difficulty. It took us a day to cross because of the swift current.

On the other side, about 200 [Timucuan] Indians moved toward us. The Govenor went to meet them and talked in signs. They gestured so menacingly that we fell upon them and seized five or six, who led us to their houses half a league away. There we found quite a quantity of corn ripe for plucking. To our Lord we lifted infinite thanks for succoring us, who were yet young in trials, in our ex-tremity; we were weak from hunger and weary.

The third day after our arrival here, the Comptroller, Inspector, and I together petitioned the Governor to send out a scouting party to seek a harbor, the Indians having told us the sea was not far off. He said to stop talking of the sea, it was remote; but since I had been the most in-sistent, he bade me go look for a port and take forty foot.

So next day [May 18] I set forth with Captain Alonso del Castillo and forty men of his company.

At noon we came upon sandy patches which seemed to stretch far inland. We walked about a league and a half [two leagues, according to the *Joint Report*], wading nearly knee-deep in water, shells cutting our feet badly. Thus with great trouble we reached the river we had first crossed and which emptied into this bay. Unequipped for crossing it, we reported back to the Governor that we would have to re-ford the big river at the place we had first gone over it, to get to the coast and ascertain if the bay had a harbor.

He sent Captain Valenzuela next day with sixty foot [forty, according to the *Joint Report*] and six horse to re-cross the river and follow its course to the sea to see whether a harbor lay there.

Valenzuela returned in two days to report that he had found the bay [the mouth of the Suwannee] but only a knee-deep, shallow expanse with no harbor. He saw five or six canoes passing from one side to the other full of many-plumed Indians.

On this intelligence, we next day resumed our dogged quest of Apalachen, using the captive Indians as guides. Thus we went until June 17 without seeing a native who would let us catch up to him.

Then on this 17th, there appeared in front of us a chief in a painted deerskin riding the back of another Indian, musicians playing reed flutes walking before, and a train of many subjects attending him. He dismounted where the Governor stood and stayed an hour. We apprised him by signs that we were on our way to Apalachen. His signs seemed to us to mean that he was an enemy of the Apalachee and would accompany us against them. We gave him beads, little bells, and other trinkets, and he gave the Governor the deerskin he wore. When he turned back, we followed.

That night we came to a wide, deep, swift river [the Apalachicola], which we did not dare cross with rafts, so constructed a canoe. Again we were a whole day getting over. Had the Indians wished to oppose us, they had a golden opportunity here; even with their help we had a hard time.

One of the mounted men, Juan Velásquez, a native of Cuéllar, impatiently rode into the river. The violent current swept him from his saddle. He grabbed the reins but drowned with the horse. The subjects of that chief—whose name turned out to be Dulchanchellin—found the body of the beast and told us where in the stream below we likely would find the body of Cuéllar. They went to look for it.

This death hit us hard, for until now not a man had been lost. The horse, meanwhile, furnished a supper for many that night.

The following day we made the chief's village, where he gave us corn. In the night, one of the Christians who had gone for water got shot with an arrow, but God pleased to spare him hurt. All the Indians fled overnight, as we discovered on pulling out next day.

They began to reappear, however, as we filed along. Apparently they had prepared for battle but, though we called to them, they withdrew and fell in behind us on the trail. The Governor left some cavalry in ambush, who surprised the natives about to pass and seized three or four, whom we kept for guides.

They led us through a difficult and marvelous country of vast forests, the trees astonishingly high. So many of them had fallen that continual detours made the march laborious. Many of the trees still standing had been riven from top to bottom by bolts of lightning, which are common in that country of frequent tempests.

So we toiled on until the day after St. John's Day [June 17], when at last we came in sight of Apalachen, unsuspected by its inhabitants. We gave many thanks to God to be near this destination, believing everything we had been told about it and expecting an immediate end of our hardships. In addition to the distance we had come over bad trails, we suffered terribly from hunger. Once in a while we did find corn, but usually had to travel seven and eight leagues without any. Also, many men developed raw wounds from the weight of their armor and other things they had to carry.

But having virtually accomplished our objective, with its assurance of plentiful gold and food, we seemed already to feel our pain and fatigue lifting.

CHAPTER 6:
The Entry into Apalachen

ON SIGHTING Apalachen [which was probably situated on or near the west bank of the Apalachicola], the Governor ordered me with nine cavalry and fifty infantry to invade the village.

The Inspector [Solís] and I accordingly marched in, to find only women and boys. The men, however, returned while we were walking about, and began discharging arrows at us. They killed the Inspector's horse and shortly fled.

We found a large stand of corn ready to pick, and a lot more already dried and stored; also many deerskins and, with them, some small, poor-quality shawls woven of thread. The women partially cover their nakedness with such garments. We also noted the bowls they grind corn in.

The village consisted of forty low, small, thatch houses set up in sheltered places for protection from the frequent storms. It was surrounded by dense woods and many little lakes, into which numerous big trees had fallen to become effective obstructions.

CHAPTER 7:
The Character of the Country

THE TERRAIN we had suffered through since first landing in Florida is mostly level, the soil sandy and stiff. Throughout are immense trees and open woods, containing nut varieties, laurels, a species called liquid-amber [sweet-gum], cedars, junipers, live-oaks, pines, red-oaks, and low palmettos like those of Castile.

Everywhere are lakes, large and small, some hard to cross because of their depth and/or profusion of fallen trees. They have sand bottoms. The lakes in the Apalachen country are far larger than any we had seen earlier.

This province has many cornfields, and houses are scattered over the countryside as at Gelves [on the Guadalquivir just south of Seville].

We saw three kinds of deer; rabbits and jackrabbits; bears and lions [panthers]; and other wild animals, including one [the opossum] which carries its young in a pouch on its belly until they are big enough to find food by themselves; but, even then, if someone approaches while they are foraging, the mother will not run before the little ones get into her pouch. [Evidently the expeditionaries saw no alligators.]

The country is very cold [rare for June days in Florida]. It has fine pastures for cattle. The wide variety of birds in abundance includes geese, ducks, royal drakes, ibises, egrets, herons, partridges, falcons, marsh-hawks, sparrowhawks, goshawks, and numerous other fowl. [Why, then, did the soldiers do no hunting?]

CHAPTER 8:

Adventures in and out of Apalachen

TWO HOURS after we arrived in Apalachen, the Indians who had fled returned in peace to ask the release of their women and children. We released them. The Governor, however, continued to hold one of their *caciques* [chiefs], whereupon they grew agitated and attacked us the next day.

'They worked so fast, with such daring, that they fired

the very houses we occupied. We sallied out after them but they fled to nearby swamps which, together with the big cornfields, kept us from harming them except for one Indian we killed.

The day after that, Indians from a village on the opposite side of the lake attacked us in the same way, escaping the same way, again losing a single man.

We stayed 25 days [26, according to the *Joint Report*] in Apalachen, during which time we made three reconnaissances, finding the country sparsely populated and hard to get through because of swamps, woods, and lakes. The *cacique,* as well as the other Indians we had been holding, confirmed our own observations when we asked them about their country. (The Indians we captured on our way to Apalachen were neighbors and enemies of the Apalachee.) Interrogated separately, they each said that Apalachen was the biggest town in the region, that farther in, the inhabitants were fewer, more scattered, and far poorer, and that large lakes, dense forests, and vast deserts and barrens awaited us in the interior.

When we asked about the country to the south, they said that nine days in that direction lay the village of Aute, where the people—their friends—had plenty of corn, beans, and melons—also fish, being near the sea.

Taking everything into consideration—the poverty of the land and unfavorable reports of the people, etc.; the constant guerilla tactics of the Indians, wounding our people and horses with impunity from the cover of the lakes whenever they went for water; and killing a *cacique* of Tezcuco [an Aztec prince] whom the Commissary had brought with him—we decided to strike for the sea and this Aute we had been hearing about. We got there in five days [a statement contradicted shortly].

The first day out [July 19 or 20] we negotiated lakes and trails without seeing a single native. But on the second day, while chest-deep in the middle of a lake which hidden logs helped make difficult to cross, a band of Indians, concealed behind groves and fallen timber, wounded quite a few men and horses and captured our guide, before we could get through the water.

They pressed after us, intending to dispute the narrow passage, but when we turned on them, they fled to the safety of the lake whence their arrows continued to hit men and beasts. The Governor commanded our cavalry to dismount and charge the Indians afoot. The Comptroller [Enríquez] dismounted and charged with them. The Indians retreated into the lake, and we gained the passage.

Good armor did no good against arrows in this skirmish. There were men who swore they had seen two red oaks, each the thickness of a man's calf, pierced from side to side by arrows this day; which is no wonder when you consider the power and skill the Indians can deliver them with. I myself saw an arrow buried half a foot in a poplar trunk.

All the Indians we had so far seen in Florida had been archers. They loomed big and naked and from a distance looked like giants. They were handsomely proportioned, lean, agile, and strong. Their bows were as thick as an arm, six or seven feet long, accurate at 200 paces.

We got through this passage only to come upon a worse one, half a league long, a league away. But the Indians had expended all their arrows at the first place, so dared not attack now.

Working through yet another such passage the following day, I detected tracks ahead and notified the Governor in the rearguard. The ambush that did develop found us ready and proved harmless. But the Indians pursued us onto the open plain. We wheeled in a double attack back to the woods, killing two warriors before we could no longer get at the band. I ended up wounded, along with two or three other Christians.

CHAPTER 9:
The Ominous Note at Aute

So WE marched on for eight days, meeting no resistance until we came within a league of our immediate objective. Then, while we ambled along unsuspectingly, Indians surprised our rear. An *hidalgo* named Avellaneda, a member of the rearguard who had already passed the point of ambush when the attack broke, heard his servant-lad cry out and turned back to assist when, just at that moment, an arrow plunged almost all the way through his neck at the edge of his cuirass, so that he died presently.

We carried him to Aute, where we arrived at the end of nine days out of Apalachen. [Aute, as later French maps concur, appears to have lain a short distance above the mouth of the Apalachicola.]

We found the village deserted and all the houses burned. But corn, squash, and beans—all beginning to ripen—were plentiful. We rested there two days.

Then the Governor urged me to locate the sea, which was supposed to be so near and which we felt we had approached because of the big river we came upon and named Río de la Magdalena [doubtless the Apalachicola].

So I went forth the following day, with the Commissary, the captain Castillo, Andrés Dorantes, seven others on horseback, and fifty afoot. We traveled till the hour of vespers, when we reached an inlet of the sea. Oysters abounded, to the joy of the hungry men, and we gave thanks to God for having brought us here.

The next morning [August 1] I despatched twenty men to explore the coast. They came back the night of their second day out and reported that these inlets and bays were enormous and cut so far inland that it would be a major undertaking to investigate them properly, also that the coast of the open sea lay yet a long way off.

In view of this intelligence and of our limited means, I went back to the Governor. We found him and many others sick. The Indians had attacked the night before and, because of this illness, the soldiers had been desperately hard put. One horse had been killed. I reported on my trip and the discouraging nature of the country. We stayed where we were that day.

CHAPTER 10:
Our Departure from Aute

THE NEXT MORNING [August 3] we quit Aute and made it to the place I had just visited. The journey was extremely arduous. We did not have horses enough to carry the sick, who kept getting worse every day, and we knew no cure for the disease [undoubtedly malaria, probably complicated by dysentery].

By the time we reached my previous campsite, it was painfully clear to all that we were unprepared to go further. Had we been prepared, we still did not know where to go; and the men could not move, most of them lying prone and those able to stand to duty very few. I will not prolong this unpleasantness; but you can imagine what it would be like in a strange, remote land, destitute of means either to remain or to get out. Our most reliable help was God our Lord; we had not wavered in this conviction.

But now something happened worse than anything that had gone before. The majority of the cavalry plotted to desert, figuring they stood a better chance if unencumbered by the prostrated Governor and largely prostrated infantry.

Since, however, many of the cavalry were *hidalgos* and well-bred persons, they could not but inform the Governor and Your Majesty's officers. We remonstrated with the plotters on the enormity of their notion until they relented and agreed to share the common fate, whatever it might be. The Governor then called them all into his presence and asked their advice, one man at a time, on how to escape that dismal country.

A third of our force had fallen seriously ill and was growing worse by the hour. We felt certain we would all be stricken, with death the one foreseeable way out; and in such a place, death seemed all the more terrible. Considering our experiences, our prospects, and various plans, we finally concluded to undertake the formidable project of constructing vessels to float away in.

This appeared impossible, since none of us knew how to build ships, and we had no tools, iron, forge, oakum, pitch, or rigging, or any of the indispensable items, or anybody to instruct us. Worse still, we had no food to sustain workers. At this impasse, we agreed to consider the matter deeper and ended our parley for the day, each going his way, commending our future to God our Lord.

CHAPTER 11:
The Building of the Barges and Our
Departure from the Bay

IT WAS HIS will that next day one of our men should come saying he could make wooden pipes and deerskin bellows. Having reached that point where any hope of relief is seized upon, we bade him commence. We also instigated the making of nails, saws, axes, and other tools we needed out of the stirrups, spurs, crossbows, and other of our equipment containing iron.

For food while the work proceeded, we decided to make four forays into Aute with every man and horse able to go, and to kill one of our horses every third day to divide among the workers and the sick. Our forays went off as planned. In spite of armed resistance, they netted as much as 400 *fanegas* [about 100 bushels] of corn.

We had stacks of palmettos gathered, and their husks and fibers twisted and otherwise prepared as a substitute for oakum. A Greek, Don Teodoro, made pitch from certain pine resins. Even though we had only one carpenter, work proceeded so rapidly from August 4, when it began, that by September 20 five barges, each 22 elbow-lengths [30 to 32 feet long], caulked with palmetto oakum and tarred with pine-pitch, were finished.

From palmetto husks, also horse tails and manes, we braided ropes and rigging; from our shirts we made sails; and from junipers, oars. Such was the country our sins had cast us in that only the most persistent search turned up stones large enough for ballast and anchors. Before this, we had not seen a stone in the whole region. We flayed the horses' legs, tanned the skin, and made leather water-bottles.

Twice in this time, when some of our men went to the coves for shellfish, Indians ambushed them, killing ten men in plain sight of the camp before we could do anything about it. We found their bodies pierced all the way through, although some of them wore good armor. I have already mentioned the power and precision of the Indian archery.

Our pilots estimated, under oath, that from the bay we had named The Cross [their first Florida campsite] we had come approximately 280 leagues to this place. In that entire space, by the way, we had seen not a single mountain nor heard of any.

Before we embarked, we lost forty men from disease and hunger, in addition to those killed by Indians. By September 22 all but one of the horses had been consumed. That is the day we embarked [after consuming this last horse], in the following order: the Governor's barge, with 49 men; the barge entrusted to the Comptroller and Commissary, also with 49 men; a third barge in charge of Captain Alonso del Castillo and Andrés Dorantes, with 48 men; another with 47 under Captains Téllez and Peñalosa; and the final barge, which the Governor assigned to the Inspector [Solís] and me, with 49 men.

When clothing and supplies were loaded, the sides of the barges remained hardly half a foot above water; and we were jammed in too tight to move. Such is the power of necessity that we should thus hazard a turbulent sea, none of us knowing anything about navigation.

CHAPTER 12:

The First Month at Sea
after Departing the Bay of Horses

THE HAVEN we set out from we gave the name *Vaya de Cavallos* [Bay of Horses]. [Twelve years later, Indians led a detachment of De Soto's expedition to this cove of Apalachicola Bay, where scattered charcoal, hollowed-out logs that had been used for water troughs, etc., could still be seen.]

We sailed seven days among those waist-deep sounds without seeing any sign of the coast of the open sea. At the end of the seventh day we came to an island [probably St. Vincent's], close to the main. From my lead barge we saw five canoes approaching. When we went after them, the Indians abandoned them to us at the island. The other barges passed mine and stopped ahead at some houses on the island, where we found a lot of mullet and dried eggs of these fish, which were a grateful relief. After this repast, we proceeded a couple of leagues to a strait we discovered between the island and the coast which we named Sant Miguel [Saint Michael], its being that saint's day [September 29].

We passed through the strait and beached on the coast of the open sea. There we made sideboards out of the canoes I had confiscated, to raise our gunwales another half foot above water level.

Then we resumed our voyage, coasting [westward] toward the River of Palms [presumably thinking it closer or more certainly findable than their own ships to the south], our hunger and thirst growing daily more intense because our scant provisions were nearly exhausted and the water-bottles we had made had rotted. We wove in and out of occasional bays, which stretched far inland, but found them all shallow and dangerous.

For thirty days we went on like this, every once in a while catching sight of Indian fishermen—a poor, miserable lot.

The night of the thirtieth day, when our want of water had become insupportable, we heard a canoe coming. We stopped when we could make it out but, although we called, it went on. The night was too dark for pursuit, so we kept our course. Dawn brought us to a little island, where we touched to look for water, but there was none.

While we lay [in the lee] there at anchor, a great storm broke over us. For six days while it raged we dared not put out to sea. Its already having been five days since we had drunk, at the time the storm erupted, our extreme thirst forced us to drink salt water. Some drank so unrestrainedly that five suddenly died.

I state this briefly because I think it superfluous to tell in detail what we went through in those circumstances. Considering where we were and how little hope we had of relief, you may sufficiently imagine our sufferings.

Our thirst was killing us; the salt water was killing us. Rather than succumb right there, we commended ourselves to God, and put forth into the perilous sea as the storm still raged. We headed in the direction of the canoe we had seen the night we came here [back, off the Alabama coast]. The waves overwhelmed our barge many

times this day, and none of us doubted that his death
would come any minute.

CHAPTER 13:
Treachery in the Night Ashore

IT WAS the will of God, Who often shows His favor in
the hour of total despair, that as we doubled a point of
land at sunset we found ourselves sheltered in calm
waters [apparently near Pensacola]; and many canoes of
big, well-built Indians—unarmed—came out to speak,
then paddled back ahead of us.

We followed them to their houses at the water's edge
close by, and stepped ashore. In front of the dwellings
stood many clay jars of water and a great quantity of
cooked fish, all of which the *cacique* of this land offered
our Governor before leading us to his "palace." Their
dwellings were made of mats and, so far as we could tell,
were not movable. When we [officers] entered the *cacique's* palace, he regaled us with fish. We gave him some
of the corn we had brought, which his people ate in our
presence and asked for more. We gave them more. The
Governor also presented the *cacique* some trinkets.

In the middle of the night, the Indians fell on us without warning—not only the Governor's party in the *cacique's* lodge, but also our sick men strewn on the beach.
[The *Joint Report* says three men were killed]. The Governor got hit in the face with a rock. Some of us grabbed
the *cacique*, but a group of Indians retrieved him, leaving
us holding his robe of civet-marten skins.

(These are the finest skins in the world, I believe. Their
fragrance seems like amber and musk and can be smelled
a long way off. We saw other robes there, but none to
match this one.)

Those of us in the vicinity where the Governor got

hurt managed to put him in his barge and to hasten all but fifty of our force aboard theirs. The fifty stood guard high up on the beach. Three times that night the Indians attacked, with such ferocity as to force us back more than a stone's throw each time.

Not one of us escaped injury. I was wounded in the face. If the Indians had had more than their few arrows, they undoubtedly would have done us serious harm. At their third onset, Captains Dorantes, Peñalosa, and Téllez with fifteen men ambushed their rear; at which the aggressors broke and fled.

CHAPTER 14:
The Disappearance of the Greek

NEXT MORNING [October 28] I broke up thirty of their canoes, which we used for fire; the north wind, which raised yet another storm, confined us to land in the cold. When the storm subsided, we returned to sea, navigating three days [three or four, says the *Joint Report*]. We had only a few containers to carry water, so could take but a little supply. Soon we were reduced again to the last extremity.

Continuing along the coast, we entered an estuary [Mobile Bay] where we saw a canoe of Indians coming toward us. We hailed them and, when they drew close to the Governor's boat, he asked for water. They showed themselves willing to get some if we furnished containers. That Greek, Doroteo Teodoro, whom I spoke of before, said he would go, too. The Governor and others failed to dissuade him. He took along a Negro, and the Indians left two of their number as hostages.

It was night when the Indians returned, without water in the containers and without the Christians.

When these returning Indians spoke to our two hostages,

the latter started to dive into the water; but some of our soldiers held them back in the barge. The canoe sped away, leaving us very confused and dejected over the loss of our comrades.

[De Soto's soldiers some twelve years later learned from Indians in this vicinity of the arrival of the barges in need of water, and of the two men who had remained behind. The Indians produced a dagger that had belonged to Teodoro. One suspects that Teodoro insisted on accompanying the canoemen for water because he thought it his best hope to survive; i.e. he had no intention of returning to the barges. He and his servant may, in fact, have lived for some time longer and migrated as slaves to tribes farther inland].

CHAPTER 15:
The Indian Assault and the
Arrival at a Great River

WITH MORNING came Indians in many canoes [twenty— Joint Report], calling on us to give up our two hostages. The Governor replied that he would when the Indians brought the two Christians.

Five or six chiefs were distinguishable in the array of natives, who looked comelier, more commanding, and better disciplined than any Indians we had yet seen, although not as big as some spoken of before. Their hair hung loose and very long, and they wore marten robes like those we had lately taken, except that some of the robes exhibited a strange combination of marten and lion skin in a handsome pattern.

They entreated us to go with them, saying they would give us the Christians, water, and many other things. All the while, additional canoes kept reinforcing the first-comers, obviously bent on blocking the mouth of that inlet. This avenue closed and the country apparently hazardous to remain in, we betook ourselves back to open sea.

There the canoes and our barges floated side by side till noon. As the Indians would not return our men, we would not release theirs. They began to hurl stones and darts as us (using slings for the stones) and threatened to shoot arrows, though we saw no more than three or four bows among them. In the midst of this commotion the wind freshened and they departed.

We went on that day [two days, says the *Joint Report*] till nightfall, when my barge, which kept the lead, discovered a promontory, on the other side of which flowed a vast river [the Mississippi]. Off a little island at the point, I anchored and awaited the other barges.

CHAPTER 16:
The Splitting-Up of the Flotilla

THE GOVERNOR did not want to stop there but went into a nearby bay dotted with islets. The other barges joined him, and we found we could take fresh water from the sea, the river emptying into it in a torrent.

To parch corn—which we had eaten raw for two days now—we scrambled onto an island, but found no firewood, so decided to go to the river, one league distant behind the point. All our efforts to breast the violent current resulted only in our getting carried farther out. The north wind rose from shore to drive us the rest of the way to the high sea in spite of anything we could do. About half a league from shore we had sounded and found no bottom even at thirty fathoms, convinced that the current somehow interfered with our measurement. [True; the normal delta depth in this vicinity in the 20th century is ten fathoms, or sixty feet.]

For two days we toiled to gain the shore. Awhile before dawn of the third, we saw smoke rising at several points and worked toward it. We found ourselves in three fathoms of water, but it was still too dark to risk landing where we had seen the columns of smoke. So we held up till daylight.

When it came, the barges had lost sight of each other and I found mine floating in thirty fathoms. Keeping my course all day, to the hour of vespers, I at last sighted two other barges. As we neared them, I recognized the closer one as that of the Governor.

He asked me what I thought we should do. I said, join the barge ahead; by no means abandon her; so the three might go where God willed, together. He said that could not be done; the lead barge was too far out to sea and he wanted to get to shore. If I wished to follow him, he continued, I should order my men to the oars, since only by arm work could the land be gained. His old cohort, Captain Pantoja, had advised him thus. Pantoja claimed that if we did not make land that day, we would not in six more, by which time we would have starved.

The Governor's will clearly divulged, I took up my oar, and all my men theirs, and we rowed till nearly sunset. But, the Governor having the healthiest and strongest men in his barge, we could not keep up. I yelled to him to throw me a rope so we could stay with him. He called back that if he were to do what he hoped that night, he must not further sap his men's strength. I said that since we were too feeble to carry out his orders to follow him, he must tell me how he would that I should act. He replied that it was no longer a time when one should command another; that each must do as he thought best to save himself; that that was what he was doing now. So saying, he pulled away in his barge.

Unable to follow, I steered toward the barge at sea, which waited for me. When fairly close, I found her to be the one commanded by Captain Peñalosa and Captain Téllez.

CHAPTER 17:
A Sinking and a Landing

OUR TWO BARGES continued in company for four days, each man eating a ration of half a handful of raw corn a day. Then the other barge was lost in a storm. [The *Joint Report* says this loss occurred the day after the two barges joined.] Nothing but God's great mercy kept us from going down, too.

It was winter and bitterly cold, and we had suffered hunger and the heavy beating of the waves for many days. Next day, the men began to collapse. By sunset, all in my barge had fallen over on one another, close to death. Few were any longer conscious. Not five could stand. When night fell, only the navigator and I remained able to tend the barge. Two hours after dark he told me I must take over; he believed he was going to die that night.

So I took the tiller. After midnight I moved over to see if he were dead. He said no, in fact was better, and would steer till daylight. In that hour I would have welcomed death rather than see so many around me in such a condition. When I had returned the helm to the navigator, I lay down to rest—but without much rest, for nothing was farther from my mind than sleep.

Near dawn I seemed to hear breakers resounding; the coast lying low, they roared louder. Surprised at this, I called to the navigator, who said he thought we were coming close to land. We sounded and found ourselves in seven fathoms. The navigator felt we should stay clear of the shore till daylight; so I took an oar and pulled it on the shore side, wheeling the stern to seaward about a league out.

As we drifted into shore, a wave caught us and heaved

the barge a horseshoe-throw [about 42 feet] out of the water. The jolt when it hit brought the dead-looking men to. Seeing land at hand, they crawled through the surf to some rocks. Here we made a fire and parched some of our corn. We also found rain water. The men began to regain their senses, their locomotion, and their hope.

This day of our landing was November 6.

[Cabeza de Vaca's approximations of the days after leaving the Bay of Horses add up to eight or nine more than the 45 or 46 allowed in his inclusive dates September 22-November 6. He could have experienced the hurling ashore a week or so later than he remembered; but his track of time while battling starvation, Indians, and the periphery of a Gulf hurricane would have been understandably faulty.]

CHAPTER 18:
What Befell Oviedo with the Indians

AFTER WE ATE, I ordered Lope de Oviedo, our strongest man, to climb one of the trees not far off and ascertain the lay of the land. He complied and found out from the treetop that we were on an island. [This was Galveston Island.] He also said that the ground looked as if cattle had trampled it and therefore that this must be a country of Christians.

I sent him back for a closer look, to see if he could find any worn trails, but warned him not to risk going too far. He went and came upon a path which he followed for half a league to some empty huts. The Indians were gone to shoal-flats [to dig roots]. He took an earthen pot, a little dog, and a few mullets and started back.

We had begun to worry what might have happened to him, so I detailed another two men to check. They met

him shortly and saw three Indians with bows and arrows
following him. The Indians were calling to him and he was
gesturing them to keep coming. When he reached us, the
Indians held back and sat down on the shore.

Half an hour later a hundred bowmen [*Joint Report:*
200, with joints of cane stuck through holes in their ears]
reinforced the first three individuals. Whatever their stat-
ure, they looked like giants to us in our fright. We could
not hope to defend ourselves; not half a dozen of us could
even stand up.

The Inspector and I walked out and greeted them. They
advanced, and we did our best to placate and ingratiate.
We gave them beads and bells, and each one of them gave
us an arrow in pledge of friendship. They told us by signs
that they would return at sunrise and bring food, having
none then.

CHAPTER 19:
The Indians' Hospitality before and
after a New Calamity

As THE SUN ROSE next morning, the Indians appeared
as they promised, bringing an abundance of fish and of
certain roots which taste like nuts, some bigger than wal-
nuts, some smaller, mostly grubbed from the water with
great labor.

That evening they came again with more fish and roots
and brought their women and children to look at us. They
thought themselves rich with the little bells and beads we
gave them, and they repeated their visits on other days.

Being provided with what we needed, we thought to
embark again. It was a struggle to dig our barge out of the
sand it had sunk in, and another struggle to launch her.

For the work in the water while launching, we stripped and stowed our clothes in the craft.

Quickly clambering in and grabbing our oars, we had rowed two crossbow shots from shore when a wave inundated us. Being naked and the cold intense, we let our oars go. The next big wave capsized the barge. The Inspector [Solís] and two others held fast, but that only carried them more certainly underneath, where they drowned.

A single roll of the sea tossed the rest of the men into the rushing surf and back onto shore half-drowned.

We lost only those the barge took down; but the survivors escaped as naked as they were born, with the loss of everything we had. That was not much, but valuable to us in that bitter November cold, our bodies so emaciated we could easily count every bone and looked the very picture of death. I can say for myself that from the month of May I had eaten nothing but corn, and that sometimes raw. I never could bring myself to eat any of the horse-meat at the time our beasts were slaughtered; and fish I did not taste ten times. On top of everything else, a cruel north wind commenced to complete our killing.

The Lord willed that we should find embers while searching the remnants of our former fire. We found more wood and soon had big fires raging. Before them, with flowing tears, we prayed for mercy and pardon, each filled with pity not only for himself but for all his wretched fellows.

At sunset the Indians, not knowing we had gone, came again with food. When they saw us looking so strangely different, they turned back in alarm. I went after them calling, and they returned, though frightened. I explained to them by signs that our barge had sunk and three of our number drowned. They could see at their feet two of the dead men who had washed ashore. They could also see that the rest of us were not far from joining these two.

The Indians, understanding our full plight, sat down and lamented for half an hour so loudly they could have been heard a long way off. It was amazing to see these wild, untaught savages howling like brutes in compassion for us. It intensified my own grief at our calamity and had the same effect on the other victims.

When the cries died down, I conferred with the Christians about asking the Indians to take us to their homes. Some of our number who had been to New Spain warned that the Indians would sacrifice us to their idols. But death being surer and nearer if we stayed where we were, I went ahead and beseeched the Indians. They were delighted. They told us to tarry a little while, then they would do as we wished.

Presently thirty of them gathered loads of wood and disappeared to their huts, which were a long walk away; while we waited with the remainder until near nightfall. Then, supporting us under our arms, they hurried us from one to another of the four big fires they had built along the path. At each fire, when we regained a little warmth and strength, they took us on so swiftly our feet hardly touched ground.

Thus we made their village, where we saw they had erected a hut for us with many fires inside. An hour later they began a dance celebration that lasted all night. For us there was no joy, feasting, or sleep, as we waited the hour they should make us victims.

In the morning, when they brought us fish and roots and acted in every way hospitably, we felt reassured and somewhat lost our anxiety of the sacrificial knife.

CHAPTER 20:
News of Other Christians

THAT VERY DAY, I saw an Indian wearing a trinket which I knew we had not given. Inquiring whence it came, we learned from our hosts' signs that it had come from men like ourselves, who bivouacked farther back. At this, I sent two Christians, with two Indians for guides, to contact them.

It so happened that the latter were at that moment on their way to see us; for the Indians had told them of us as us of them. My detail met them therefore nearby.

They turned out to be Captains Andrés Dorantes and Alonso del Castillo with their entire crew [of 48]. When they came up, they were appalled at our appearance and sad that they had no other clothes than what they then wore.

They told us that their barge had capsized a league and a half from here the 5th of this month [i.e., the day before Cabeza de Vaca's barge was cast ashore] and that they escaped without losing a thing.

We decided to repair their barge, so that those who were strong enough and willing could resume the voyage, while the others stayed until their health allowed them to walk along the coast, and one day God our Lord should bring us all alike to a land of Christians.

We set directly to work but, before we could wrest the barge out of the water, Tavera, a gentleman of our company, died; and then the unseaworthy barge sank.

With most of us naked and the weather discouraging walking or swimming across rivers and coves—also with no food supply or even anything to carry one in—we resigned ourselves to remaining where we were for the winter.

We did, however, decide that four of our most robust men should set out now for Pánuco, which we believed close. Should God our Lord prosper them, they could report our destitute existence on this island. The four were: Alvaro Fernández, a Portuguese carpenter and sailor; a certain Méndez; Figueroa, an *hidalgo* from Toledo; and Astudillo of Zafra—all excellent swimmers. They took with them an Indian of the island of Auia [which presumably was the Indian name of Galveston, though another island could possibly have been meant].

CHAPTER 21:
Why We Named the Island "Doom"

WITHIN A FEW DAYS of the departure of the four Christians, the weather turned so cold and stormy that the Indians could not pull up roots; their cane contraptions for
catching fish yielded nothing; and the huts being very
open, our men began to die.

Five Christians quartered on the coast came to the ex-
tremity of eating each other. Only the body of the last one,
whom nobody was left to eat, was found unconsumed.
Their names were Sierra, Diego Lopez, Corral, Palacios,
and Gonzalo Ruiz.

The Indians were so shocked at this cannibalism that,
if they had seen it sometime earlier, they surely would
have killed every one of us. In a very short while as it
was, only fifteen of the eighty who had come survived.
[Strictly speaking, there must have been more than ninety
who made it to the island, and sixteen of them proved
later to be living].

Then half the natives died from a disease of the bowels
[doubtless infected with the soldiers' dysentery] and [the
rest] blamed us.

When they came to kill us, the Indian who kept me interceded. He said: If we had so much power of sorcery
we would not have let all but a few of our own perish;
the few left did no hurt or wrong; it would be best to leave
us alone. God our Lord be praised, they listened and relented.

We named this place *Malhado*—the "Island of Doom."

CHAPTER 22:
The Malhado Way of Life

THE PEOPLE we came to know there [Capoques and Han, as identified later in the narrative] are tall and well-built. Their only weapons are bows and arrows, which they use with great dexterity. The men bore through one of their nipples, some both, and insert a joint of cane two and a half palms long by two fingers thick. They also bore their lower lip and wear a piece of cane in it half a finger in diameter.

Their women toil incessantly.

From October to the end of February every year, which is the season these Indians live on the island, they subsist on the roots I have mentioned, which the women get from under water in November and December. Only in these two months, too, do they take fish in their cane weirs. When the fish is consumed, the roots furnish the one staple. At the end of February the islanders go into other parts to seek sustenance, for then the root is beginning to grow and is not edible.

These people love their offspring more than any in the world and treat them very mildly.

If a son dies, the whole village joins the parents and kindred in weeping. The parents set off the wails each day before dawn, again at noon, and at sunset, for one year. The funeral rites occur when the year of mourning is up. Following these rites, the survivors wash off the smoke stain of the ceremony in a symbolic purgation. All the dead are lamented this way except the aged, who merit no regrets. The dead are buried, except medicine-men, who are cremated. Everybody in the village dances and makes merry while the pyre of a medicine-man kindles, and until his bones become powder. A year later, when his rites are celebrated, the entire village again participating, this powder is presented in water for the relatives to drink.

Each man has an acknowledged wife, except the medicine-men, who may have two or three wives apiece. The several wives live together in perfect amity.

When a daughter marries, she must take everything her husband kills in hunting or catches in fishing to the house of her father, without daring to eat or to withhold any part of it, and the husband gets provided by female carrier from his father-in-law's house. Neither the bride's father nor mother may enter the son-in-law's house after the marriage, nor he theirs; and this holds for the children of the respective couples. If a man and his in-laws should chance to be walking so they would meet, they turn silently aside from each other and go a crossbow-shot out of their way, averting their glance to the ground. The woman, however, is free to fraternize with the parents and relatives of her husband. These marriage customs prevail for more than fifty leagues inland from the island.

At a house where a son or brother may die, no one goes out for food for three months, the neighbors and other relatives providing what is eaten. Because of this custom, which the Indians literally would not break to save their lives, great hunger reigned in most houses while we resided there, it being a time of repeated deaths. Those who sought food worked hard, but they could get little in that severe season. That is why the Indians who kept me left the island by canoe for oyster bays on the main.

Three months out of every year they eat nothing but oysters and drink very bad water. Wood is scarce; mosquitoes, plentiful. The houses are made of mats; their floors consist of masses of oyster shells. The natives sleep on these shells—in animal skins, those who happen to own such.

Many a time I would have to go three days without eating, as would the natives. I thought it impossible that life could be so prolonged in such protracted hunger; though afterwards I found myself in yet greater want, as shall be seen.

The [Han] Indians who had Alonso del Castillo, Andrés Dorantes, and the others of their barge who remained alive, spoke a different dialect and claimed a different descent from these I lived among. They frequented the opposite shore of the main to eat oysters, staying till the first of April, then returning.

The distance to the main is two leagues at the widest part of the channel. The island itself, which supports the two tribes commodiously, is half a league wide by five long. [Whether computing by the 2.6 or the 3.1-mile league, this is a fairly accurate estimate of the actual 1.8-mile average width of Galveston Island and the 5.4-mile maximum distance from the mainland; but the treetop estimate of the length is only about half the island's actual 29.6-mile extent.]

The inhabitants of all these parts go naked, except that the women cover some part of their persons with a wool that grows on trees [Spanish moss], and damsels dress in deerskin.

The people are generous to each other with what little they have. There is no chief. All belonging to the same lineage keep together. They speak two languages: Capoque and Han.

They have a strange custom when acquaintances [distantly separated?] meet or occasionally visit, of weeping for half an hour before they speak. This over, the one who is visited rises and gives his visitor all he has. The latter accepts it and, after a while, carries it away, often without a word. They have other strange customs, but I have told the principal and most remarkable of them. [These last six paragraphs have been transposed from the succeeding chapter.]

In April [1529] we went to the seashore and ate blackberries all month, a time of *areitos* [dance ceremonies] and *fiestas* among the Indians.

CHAPTER 23:
How We Became Medicine-Men

THE ISLANDERS wanted to make physicians of us without examination or a review of diplomas. Their method of cure is to blow on the sick, the breath and the laying-on of hands supposedly casting out the infirmity. They insisted we should do this too and be of some use to them. We scoffed at their cures and at the idea we knew how to heal. But they withheld food from us until we complied. An Indian told me I knew not whereof I spoke in saying their methods had no effect. Stones and other things growing about in the fields, he said, had a virtue whereby passing a pebble along the stomach could take away pain and heal; surely extraordinary men like us embodied such powers over nature. Hunger forced us to obey, but disclaiming any responsibility for our failure or success.

An Indian, falling sick, would send for a medicine-man, who would apply his cure. The patient would then give the medicine-man all he had and seek more from his relatives to give. The medicine-man makes incisions over the point of the pain, sucks the wound, and cauterizes it. This remedy enjoys high repute among the Indians. I have, as a matter of fact, tried it on myself with good results. The medicine-men blow on the spot they have treated, as a finishing touch, and the patient regards himself relieved.

Our method, however, was to bless the sick, breathe upon them, recite a *Pater noster* and *Ave Maria,* and pray earnestly to God our Lord for their recovery. When we concluded with the sign of the cross, He willed that our patients should directly spread the news that they had been restored to health.

64

In consequence, the Indians treated us kindly. They deprived themselves of food to give to us, and presented us skins and other tokens of gratitude.

CHAPTER 24:

My Years as a Wandering Merchant

AFTER Dorantes and Castillo returned to the island [from the Han oyster-eating season on the main], they rounded up all the surviving Christians, who were living somewhat separated from each other. They totaled fourteen. As I have said, I happened to be opposite on the main at that time participating in the Capoque blackberry-eating season. There I fell desperately ill. If anything before had given me hopes of life, this dashed them.

When the other Christians heard of my condition, they gave an Indian the wonderful robe of marten-skins we had taken from the *cacique* [in that midnight brawl near Pensacola], to bring them over to visit me. [The robe could have been, in reality, a bribe to make their getaway down the coast but, in any case, they would still need a guide to show them where the channel was shallow enough to wade, or a canoe if they were ferried.] Those who came were: Alonso del Castillo, Andrés Dorantes, [his cousin] Diego Dorantes, [Pedro de] Valdevieso [another cousin of Andrés], Estrada, Tostado, Chaves, Gutierrez, Asturiano (a priest), Diego de Huelva, Estevánico the black [a Moor from the west coast of Morocco]; and Benitez. When they reached the main, they found another of our company, Francisco de León [evidently a survivor of Cabeza de Vaca's barge, also kept by the Capoques].

The moment they had crossed; my Indians came to tell me and also brought word that Jerónimo de Alaniz [the notary] and Lope de Oviedo remained on the island. But sickness kept me from going [south] with my comrades; I did not even get to see them.

I had to stay with the Capoques more than a year. Because of the hard work they put me to, and their harsh treatment, I resolved to flee to the people of Charruco in the forests of the main. [Perhaps Cabeza de Vaca's illness bore on his change in status from a kindly treated medicine-man to a harshly treated slave; but he does not trace the transition for us. His comrades, living most of the time apart with the Han, apparently underwent the same drastic reduction in status.] My life had become unbearable. In addition to much other work, I had to grub roots in the water or from underground in the canebrakes. My fingers got so raw that if a straw touched them they would bleed. The broken canes often slashed my flesh; I had to work amidst them without benefit of clothes.

So I set to contriving how I might transfer to the forest-dwellers, who looked more propitious. My solution was to turn to trade.

[Escaping to Charruco about February 1530,] I did my best to devise ways of making my traffic profitable so I could get food and good treatment. The various Indians would beg me to go from one quarter to another for things they needed; their incessant hostilities made it impossible for them to travel cross-country or make many exchanges.

But as a neutral merchant I went into the interior as far as I pleased [the consensus is that he got as far as Oklahoma] and along the coast forty or fifty leagues [or at least, as Hallenbeck points out, between the impassable Sabine marshes to the north and perhaps not quite to Matagorda Bay to the south, where he would have learned far sooner than he did of three Spaniards who survived in that vicinity].

My principal wares were cones and other pieces of sea-snail, conchs used for cutting, sea-beads, and a fruit like a bean [from mesquite trees] which the Indians value very highly, using it for a medicine and for a ritual beverage in their dances and festivities. This is the sort of thing I carried inland. By barter I got and brought back to the coast skins, red ochre which they rub on their faces, hard canes for arrows, flint for arrowheads, with sinews and cement to attach them, and tassels of deer hair which they dye red.

This occupation suited me; I could travel where I wished, was not obliged to work, and was not a slave. Wherever I went, the Indians treated me honorably and gave me food, because they liked my commodities. They were glad to see me when I came and delighted to be brought what they wanted. I became well known; those who did not know me personally knew me by reputation and sought my acquaintance. This served my main purpose, which all the while was to determine an eventual road out.

The hardships I endured in this journeying business were long to tell—peril and privation, storms and frost, which often overtook me alone in the wilderness. By the unfailing grace of God our Lord I came forth from them all. Because of them, however, I avoided the pursuit of my business in winter, a season when, anyway, the natives retire inside their huts in a kind of stupor, incapable of exertion. [Hallenbeck reasons that Cabeza de Vaca wintered on the Trinity River or one of its western branches; the red ochre he acquired somewhere in that area is found in the woods around Nacogdoches.]

I was in this [general coastal] region nearly six years [but in this particular vicinity from early winter 1528 to early winter 1532, a merchant for perhaps 22 months], alone among the Indians and naked like them. The reason I remained so long was my intention of taking the Christian, Lope de Oviedo, away with me. His companion on the island, Alaniz, whom Castillo, Dorantes, and the rest had left behind, died soon after their departure. To get Oviedo, the last survivor there, I passed over to the island every year and pleaded with him to come with me to attempt the best way we could contrive to find Christians. Each year he put me off, saying the next we would start.

CHAPTER 25:
The Journey to the Great Bay

AT LAST, [on the fourth visit, in November 1532] I got him off, across the strait, and across four large streams on the coast [Bastrop Bayou, Brazos River, San Bernardo River, and Caney Creek]; which took some doing, because Oviedo could not swim.

So we worked along, with some Indians, until we came to a bay a league wide and uniformly deep. From its appearance we presumed it to be Espíritu Santo [the name Pineda gave Matagorda Bay in 1519; Pineda's map, with which Cabeza de Vaca was familiar, mentions the conspicuous white sandhills beyond. They were guided not across the bay but across the Colorado River which flows into it.]

We met some Indians on the other side who were on their way to visit our late hosts. They told us that three men like us lived but a couple of days from here, and said their names. We asked about the others and were told that they were all dead. Most had died of cold and hunger. But our informants' own tribe had murdered Diego Dorantes, Valdevieso, and Diego de Huelva for sport because they left one house for another; and the neighboring tribe, where Captain Dorantes now resided, had, in obedience to a dream, murdered Esquivel [who had been in the Comptroller's barge] and Méndez [one of the four excellent swimmers who had set out, back in 1528, for Pánuco]. We asked how the living Christians fared. Badly, they replied; the boys and some of the Indian men enlivened their dreary idleness by constantly kicking, cuffing, and cudgeling the three slaves; such was the life they led.

We inquired of the region ahead and its subsistence.

68

They said there was nothing to eat and that the few people [who evidently had not yet joined the nut-gathering exodus] were dying from the cold, having no skins or anything else to cover themselves with. They also told us that if we wished to see those three Christians, the Indians who had them would be coming in about two days to eat nuts [pecans] on the river bank a league from here.

So we would know they had spoken the truth about the bad treatment of our fellows, they commenced slapping and batting Oviedo and did not spare me either. They would keep throwing clods at us, too, and each of the days we waited there they would stick their arrows to our hearts and say they had a mind to kill us the way they had finished our friends. My frightened companion Oviedo said he wanted to go back with the women who had just forded the bay with us (their men having stayed some distance behind). I argued my utmost against such a craven course, but in no way could keep him.

He went back, and I remained alone with those savages. They are called Quevenes and those with whom he returned, Deaguanes. [This is the last that was ever heard of the strongest man who had sailed in Cabeza de Vaca's barge.]

CHAPTER 26:
The Coming of the Indians with
Dorantes, Castillo, and Estevánico

TWO DAYS after Lope de Oviedo departed, the Indians who had Alonso del Castillo and Andrés Dorantes reached the place we had been told of, to eat pecans. These are ground with a kind of small grain and furnish the sole subsistence of the people for two months of the year—and not every year, because the trees only bear every other year. The nut is the same size as that of Galicia; the trees are massive and numberless. [According to the *Joint Report,* these groves where the Indians began nutcracking were ten or twelve leagues above the Bay, i.e., on the lower Colorado, and tribes converged there from a distance of twenty and thirty leagues. In the course of the gathering season they worked a great distance up-river.]

An Indian [not one of those who had been manhandling Cabeza de Vaca but a recent arrival] told me secretly that the Christians had arrived at the appointed place and, if I wished to see them, to steal away to a segment of the woods which he pointed out and that there he and his relatives would pick me up as they passed by. I decided to trust him, since he spoke a dialect distinct from the others. Next day, they found me hiding in the designated place and took me along.

As we approached their abode, Andrés Dorantes came out to see who it could be; the Indians had told him a Christian was coming. When he saw me, he was terrified; for I had been considered long dead and the natives had confirmed·my demise, he said [without mentioning that he was guilty of deserting a superior officer whom he had passed by without seeing in his presumed final illness]. But we gave many thanks to be alive together. This was a day of as great joy as we ever knew.

When we got to the place Castillo was, they asked me where I might be bound. To the land of Christians, I replied, and was seeking it right now. Andrés Dorantes said that he had long entreated Castillo and Estevánico to go forward, but that they overly dreaded the many bays and rivers they would have to cross, not knowing how to swim. Thus God our Lord had preserved me through all adversities, leading me in the end to the fellowship of those who had abandoned me, that I might lead them over the bays and rivers which obstructed our progress.

They warned me that if the Indians suspected my intention of going on they would murder me; to succeed, we would have to lie quiet until the end of six months, when these Indians would migrate to another part of the country for their season of picking prickly pears. People from parts farther on would be bringing bows to barter and, after making our escape, we could accompany them on their return. Consenting to this counsel, I stayed.

The prickly pear [or tuna, the fruit of the *Opúntia* cactus,] is the size of a hen's egg, bright red and black in color, and good-tasting. The natives live solely on it three months of the year.

I was consigned as a slave to the Indian who had Dorantes. This Indian was squint-eyed; so were his wife and sons and another member of his household; so they were all, in a manner of speaking, semi-squinted. [The preceding sentence does not appear in the 1542 edition.] They were Mariames; the neighboring people who kept Castillo were Yguaces.

CHAPTER 27:

The Story of What Had Happened
to the Others

NOW I HEARD HERE how Dorantes and the eleven with him had left the island of Malhado [around late April, 1529] and stumbled upon the barge in which the Comptroller and the friars had sailed, bottom up on the seashore [at the mouth of the San Bernardo, according to data given in the *Joint Report*]; how, making their way down the coast, they had encountered four large, swift streams [the same four Cabeza de Vaca mentions crossing a few years later, though they were much higher at the season the Dorantes party passed them; the *Joint Report* specifies that Dorantes and Castillo reached the first of the four streams two leagues after gaining the mainland; the sec-

ond, three after that; and the third, three or four after
that; it was at this third that they found the remains of the
Enríquez-Suárez barge; another five or six leagues after
that they reached the fourth large stream; and in another
fifteen, ˜Matagorda Bay, which they too recognized as
Pineda's Espíritu Santo]; and how four of their number
drowned when the rafts they were using to cross [the
Brazos, or second large stream, according to the *Joint
Report*] swept out to sea. [The *Joint Report* says two men
drowned thus.]

So they proceeded [another four days (*Joint Report*)]
to the bay [which the *Joint Report* notes was nearly a
league across and formed a point of land jutting nearly
four leagues into the sea toward Pánuco, with great white
sand dunes visible a long distance inland; which bay]
they got over [in two days' time] with extreme difficulty.
[Instead of taking the trail that cut inside that long point
of land—Matagorda Peninsula—via the north shore of
the bay and then across the Colorado, as Cabeza de
Vaca's guides had directed him and Oviedo, the guideless
Dorantes party kept right along the coast until they found
themselves stranded at the tip of Matagorda Peninsula,
whence they made their way in a broken canoe the *Joint
Report* says they found there, through Cavallo Pass in
the middle of the vast bay.] By the time they reached
this inlet [Matagorda Bay], they had lost two men in the
sixty leagues they had traveled [nearer thirty-five leagues, or
a little more than one hundred miles from Galveston Island, but faintness always made the distances seem about
double what they were]; the remainder were nearly dead,
having eaten nothing the whole while but crabs and kelp.

Walking along the peninsula at this bay, they found
Indians eating blackberries who, at sight of the sojourners,
withdrew to a cape opposite. While the Dorantes party
were wracking their brains for some way to get across the
water, they saw an Indian crossing over toward them and,
with him, a Christian, whom they recognized as Figueroa
[of Toledo], one of the four we had sent ahead from the
Island of Doom [in 1528].

CHAPTER 28:
Figueroa's Further Story of What Had Happened to the Others

FIGUEROA recounted [to Dorantes, Castillo, and the eight or nine men with them there on the peninsula] how he and his three companions had got as far as that place [Matagorda Bay] when two of them [Fernández, the Portuguese sailor, and Astudillo, the native of Zafra] and the Indian [of Auia] died of cold and hunger; it was the middle of the winter.

The Indians took Figueroa and Méndez. Méndez fled, in the direction of Pánuco; but the Indians gave chase and, when they caught him, put him to death.

While living with these Indians, Figueroa learned from them that another Christian who had come over [Matagorda Bay], but from the opposite side, was among the Mariames. Figueroa found him among the Quevenes. He turned out to be Hernando de Esquivel, a native of Badajoz, who had sailed in the Commissary's barge. From him Figueroa learned what had become of the Governor, the Comptroller, and the others, as follows.

The Comptroller [Enríquez] and the friars capsized and lost their barge against the rocks at the mouth of a river [the San Bernardo, November 1528], and proceeded down the coast afoot. The Governor passed by, landed the men in his barge and coasted on while they walked; took them back on at the great [Matagorda] bay, deposited them on the other side, returned for the Enríquez-Suárez hikers, and deposited them with the others on the south rim.

There the Governor revoked the Comptroller's commission as lieutenant and reassigned it to Captain Pantoja.

That night, Narváez stayed aboard his barge, with a cock-
swain and a sick page. There was no food on board [or,
for that matter, on shore]. At midnight, a strong north
wind carried the barge, which had only a stone for an
anchor, unobserved to sea. And that was the last that was
known of the Commander. [It is possible, as Hallenbeck
detects, that the Governor deliberately deserted his charges
and headed on for Pánuco, which he never reached.]

The rest kept going along the coast. Impeded by another
wide expanse of water [San Antonio Bay], they made
rafts with much labor and crossed. Farther on, they came
to a point of woods in the water where [some Quevene]
Indians, at sight of them, stowed their [rolled-up mat]
houses in their canoes and fled to the opposite side [evi-
dently of Copano Bay, into which the Blanco and Aransas
empty]. Considering the season—it was still November
[1528]—the Christians stopped at this wood, where they
found water and fuel, some crabs and shellfish.

One by one they began to die of cold and hunger; and
Pantoja, now lieutenant governor, used them severely. At
last, Sotomayor could take no more of his high-handed-
ness. Sotomayor was a brother of Vasco Porcallo of Cuba
and had joined the expedition as campmaster. In a fight,
he clubbed Pantoja, who died instantly.

Thus the number went on diminishing. The living dried
the flesh of those who died. The last to die was Sotomayor.
Esquivel, by feeding on the corpse, was able to stay alive
until the first of March, when one of the Indians who had
fled returned to see if anybody might still be alive and
took Esquivel with him.

Esquivel was in this native's possession when Figueroa
found him and learned what had just been related. He
pleaded with Esquivel to seek the way to Pánuco with
him, but Esquivel would not consent. He said he understood from the friars that Pánuco had already been passed.
So he stayed there and Figueroa went back up to that part
of the coast where he was accustomed to live.

Figueroa, in concluding his tale, said that if his listeners
should at any time go in that direction, they too could see

Esquivel; for Figueroa knew that he had fled from the Indian who had him to the neighboring Mariames.

[The *Joint Report* gives an extensive but confusing account of what happened after Figueroa had finished his story. The likeliest squaring of the details would be something like this: The Indian who had brought Figueroa to the peninsula would not allow him to tarry longer; but this Indian and any others who paddled up promised the famished Dorantes party fish if they would come for it, the promise including transportation back. The priest, Asturiano, and an unidentified young man, being the only ones who could swim, accompanied Figueroa and the canoemen. But when they reached the tribal village, apparently in the northern part of the bay, the Indians kept the former two as well as Figueroa with them. The remaining eight of the Dorantes party got across to the head of the bay in the broken canoe they found at the tip of the peninsula, though it is possible they had already got across when Figueroa first found them. They, at any rate, spent either the rest of the day they had talked with Figueroa, or the day following, eating wild blackberries; and the day after that, the Indians who had Figueroa and the other two Christians stowed their houses and repaired to that vicinity to eat blackberries, too. They treated the Dorantes party cavalierly, helping themselves to anything they wanted from them almost by force. But these Indians did at last relent and take the Dorantes party to their newly set-up houses where they proferred a small amount of fish at dark, and the next day shared part of a fresh catch. Figueroa was able, under close guard, to inform his friends that Esquivel had been killed attempting to escape, and that this had happened a month after Figueroa had seen him (thus within the last few days of this May 1629). The itinerant Indians moved away once again, taking the three Christians with them and saying they would be back soon.]

After Figueroa finished telling his story, he and the Asturian broke from the Indians farther on [obviously some time after they had been carried away]. When the

Indians [who then had or shortly would have the Dorantes group] found out about this escape, they went after the fugitives and beat them severely. They stripped the Asturian and pierced his arm with an arrow. He and Figueroa did, however, finally make good their flight.

CHAPTER 29:

Last Up-Dating on the Fate of the Others

THE REMAINING [eight] Christians prevailed on the Indians to receive them as slaves. [The *Joint Report* says that they first lingered with the fishing and blackberry-picking Indians who did not migrate with the group who had Figueroa, the priest, and the young swimmer; but that these hosts tired of seeking food for their guests and turned five of them away, telling them to go to some Indians to be found in another bay six leagues farther on. Three of these five—Alonso del Castillo, Pedro de Valdevieso, and Diego de Huelva went there (San Antonio Bay?) and stayed a long time. Diego Dorantes and the unidentified fifth man sought relief elsewhere, down near the coast. The two *hidalgos* (who would be Andrés Dorantes and Castillo; therefore Castillo is probably listed mistakenly as one of the group of three who left) and the Negro (Estevánico, who belonged to Andrés) stayed at the first place, carrying backloads of wood and water as slaves. But in only three or four days, they too were turned away. They wandered lost for some time, without hope of relief. One night they were robbed of their clothes.

It was while trudging naked among the coastal marshes that they came upon the dead bodies of Diego Dorantes and his companion. Andrés and his two companions continued along that path until they found some Quevenes, with whom they remained.

These Indians (members of whose tribe manhandled Cabeza de Vaca and Oviedo when the latter crossed the lower Colorado a few years later) lived close to the shore, but on the opposite side of the bay where Valdevieso and his two companions had gone. Valdevieso came over to report to the newcomers that the swimmers (Figúeroa, the priest, and the young man) had passed in that direction, stripped and badly bruised about the head with sticks because of leaving. But they had gone on anyway, having taken an oath never to stop, even if death stood in their path, before reaching a country of Christians. Dorantes saw in the *ranchería* where he was kept the clothes of the priest and of one of the swimmers, with a breviary or prayer book. Valdevieso went back to the other side of this bay, and a couple of days later was killed because he wanted to flee. Not long after that, Huelva was killed because he forsook one lodge-house for another.]

In the service of the Indians, the Dorantes party [following the abduction of the two swimmers] were abused as slaves never were, nor men in any condition have ever been. Not content with frequently buffeting them, striking them with sticks, and pulling out their beards for amusement, they killed three of the six for only going from one house to another. These were the persons I have named before: Diego Dorantes, Valdevieso, and Diego de Huelva. The three who remained looked forward to the same fate. [*Joint Report:* The Christians (in two groups on opposite sides of the bay) were there made slaves and forced to serve with more cruelty than the Moor would have used. Besides going stark naked and barefoot over the coast which burned like fire in summertime, their constant occupation was bringing wood and water on their backs, or whatever the Indians needed, and dragging canoes over marshy ground in hot weather. Andrés Dorantes lived in constant dread of being killed.]

Not to endure this life, Dorantes fled [at noon one day in August 1530, according to the *Joint Report*, back more than twenty leagues to a river near Matagorda Bay] to the Mariames, the people among whom Esquivel had last tarried. They told him that Esquivel had wanted to run away because a woman dreamed that a son of hers would kill him; and that they overtook and slew him. They showed Dorantes his sword, beads, book, and other of his effects.

[Now only the men of the Téllez-Peñalosa barge remained unaccounted for. Cabeza de Vaca heard about them in the summer of 1535, as he reports farther on.]

CHAPTER 30:

The Life of the Mariames and Yguaces

THUS ENTHRALLED to their custom, they take life, destroying even their male children on account of dreams. [Obedience to dreams, according to Dorantes in the *Joint Report,* is the one superstition of these people. He said he had witnessed the killing or burying alive of eleven or twelve boys; rarely, he added, do they let a girl live.]

They cast away their daughters at birth; the dogs eat them. They say they do this because all the nations of the region are their enemies, with whom they war ceaselessly; and that if they were to marry off their daughters, the daughters would multiply their enemies until the latter overcame and enslaved the Mariames, who thus preferred to annihilate all daughters than risk their reproduction of a single enemy. We asked why they did not themselves marry these girls. They said that marrying relatives would be a disgusting thing; it was far better to kill them than give them to either kin or foe.

This is also the practice of their neighbors, the Yguaces, but of no other people of that region. To marry, men buy wives from their enemies, the price of a wife being the best bow that can be got, together with two arrows or, should the suitor happen to have no bow, a net a fathom square. Couples kill their own male children and buy those of strangers. A marriage lasts no longer than suits the parties; they separate on the slightest pretext. Dorantes lived a few days [months] among this people [the Quevenes] and then escaped [to the Mariames]. [The Quevenes, a fish- and blackberry-eating tribe, as the *Joint Report* makes clear, seem to have been an offshoot of the Mariames, with whom Cabeza de Vaca here tends to lump them.]

Castillo and Estevánico went inland to the Yguaces. These people are invariably good archers and well formed, though smaller than the [Capoque and Han] Indians we left. They have a nipple and a lip bored.

Two or three kinds of root comprise their basic diet, and they dig for them anywhere for the distance of two or three leagues. Digging for them is hard work. Want is so acute that these people cannot get through the year without roots which, however, make poor food and gripe the stomach. The roots have to be roasted for two days, but many still stay bitter.

Occasionally, these Indians kill deer [antelope] and take fish; but the quantity is so small and famine so prevalent that they eat spiders and ant eggs [pupae], worms, lizards, salamanders, snakes, and poisonous vipers; also earth and wood—anything, including deer dung and other matter I omit. I honestly believe that if there were stones in that land they would eat them. They save the bones of fish they consume, of snakes and other animals, so they can afterwards pulverize and eat them, too.

The men bear no burdens. Anything of weight is borne by women and old men, the people least esteemed. They do not love their children as do the Capoques. Some among them are accustomed to sin against nature. The women work very hard and protractedly. They get only six hours' rest out of twenty-four, spending the wee hours heating the ovens to bake roots. They begin digging at daybreak and hauling wood and water to their houses, etc.

The majority of the people are great thieves. Free as they are to divide with each other, at the turn of a head even a son or a father will take what he can. They are great liars, also great drunkards by use of a certain [cactus] liquor.

These Indians are so used to running that, without rest, they follow a deer from morning to night. In this way they kill many. They wear the deer down and then sometimes overtake them in a race.

Their houses are of matting placed on four hoops. They are carried on the back [of the women], and the people move every two or three days in search of food. Nothing is planted for support.

They are a merry people, considering the hunger they suffer. They never skip their *fiestas* and *areitos*. To them the happiest time of year is the season of eating prickly pears. They go in no want then and pass the whole time dancing and eating, day and night. They squeeze out the juice of the prickly pears, then open and set them to dry. The dried fruit, something like figs, is put in hampers to be eaten on the way back. The peel is beaten to powder.

Many times while we were among this people and there was nothing to eat for three or four days, they would try to revive our spirits by telling us not to be sad; soon there would be prickly pears in plenty; we would drink the juice, our bellies would get big, and we would be content. From the first talk like this we heard to the first ripening of the prickly pears was an interval of five or six months. This period having lapsed and the season come, we went to eat the fruit.

We found mosquitoes of three sorts, all abundant in every part of the region. They poison and inflame and, through most of the summer, exasperated us. For protection, we encircled ourselves with smudge fires of rotten and wet wood. We did little else all night than shed tears from the smoke of this remedy, besides roasting from the intense heat of the many fires. If at any time we took refuge to the seaside and fell asleep, we were reminded with blows to feed the fires. The Indians of the interior have another intolerable method, even worse than the one I have just mentioned, which is to fire the plains and forests within reach with brands, both to drive the mosquitoes away and at the same time drive lizards and like things from the earth to eat.

They also kill deer [antelope] by encircling fires; deprived of pasturage, the animals are forced to seek it where the Indians may trap them. The Indians encamp only where they can find wood and water. Sometimes everybody carries loads of these to hunt deer, which usually are found where wood and water are not. The Indians kill all the deer and other animals they can the day of their arrival, then consume the whole of their water and wood in cooking and smudge fires. They tarry the next day to get something to sustain their homeward hike. By the time they go, the ravages of those insects make them look as if they had the affliction of holy Lazarus.

In this way they appease their hunger two or three times a year, at the cost I have stated. I can declare from sad experience that there is no torment in the world to equal it.

Inland are many deer, fowl, and beasts other than those I have spoken of. Cattle [buffalo] come as far as here [evidently the vicinity of Austin, the southernmost range of the buffalo and the area of the Mariames' wintry deer hunts]. Three times I have seen and eaten them. I think they are about the size of those in Spain. They have small horns like the cows of Morocco; their hair is very long and flocky like merinos'. Some are tawny, others black. In my opinion the meat is finer and fatter than the beef of this country. The Indians make blankets out of the skins of cows not full grown; and shoes and shields from the full-grown. These cattle come from as far away as the seacoast of Florida, from a northerly direction, and range over a tract of more than 400 leagues. Throughout this whole range, the people who dwell nearby descend and live upon them and distribute an incredible number of hides into the interior.

CHAPTER 31:
The Tribal Split and
News of the Remaining Barge

WHEN THE six months I had been biding my time were
up, the Indians proceeded to the prickly pears thirty
leagues away [the vicinity of San Antonio], and the moment to execute our escape plan drew nigh. [This migra-
tion must have occurred in August 1533.] When we drew
near the point of flight, our Indian masters quarreled over
a woman. After a scuffle in which heads were bruised
with fists and sticks, each took his lodge and went his own
way. So we Christians found ourselves separated with no
means of reuniting for another year.

During this year my lot was hard, as much from hunger
as harsh treatment. Three times I had to run from my
masters, who came after me with intent to kill; but each
time, God our Lord preserved me. When the prickly pear
season at last arrived again, we Christians came together
with the aggregation of all the tribe in the cactus thickets.

We set a time for our escape, but that same day the
Indians dispersed to different locales of the cactus country. I told my comrades I would wait for them at a certain spot among the prickly pear plants until the full moon.
This day I was speaking to them was the new moon, September 1 [1534, in which year the new moon actually
occurred on September 8]. I said that if they did not appear by the time the moon was full, I would go on alone.
So we parted, each going with his Indian group.

On the thirteenth day of the moon, Andrés Dorantes
came with Estevánico and told me they had left Castillo
with other Indians nearby, called Anagados [Lanegados,
1555 edition]; that they had encountered great obstacles

82

and got lost; that tomorrow the Mariames were going to move to the place where Castillo was and unite in friendship with this tribe which held him, having heretofore been at war with them. In this way we would recover Castillo.

The thirst we had all the while we ate the pears, we quenched with their juice. We caught it in a hole we hollowed out in the ground [surely in rock]. When the hole was full, we drank until slaked. The juice is sweet and must-colored. The Indians collect it like this for lack of vessels. There are many kinds of prickly pear, some very good; they all seemed so to me, hunger never leaving me the leisure to discriminate.

Aside from prickly pear juice, nearly all these people drink rain water, which lies about in puddles. There are rivers; but since the Indians know no fixed abode, they have no familiar places for getting water.

Over all the region we saw vast and beautiful plains that would make good pasture. I think the land would prove very productive if developed by civilized men. We saw no mountains.

When the tribes made their juncture next day, the [Anagado] Indians told us that another people, immediately ahead of us, called Camones, who came from close to the coast, had killed the men who landed in the barge of Peñalosa and Téllez. These men arrived so feeble that they could offer no resistance even while being slain, and the Camones slew them to a man. We were shown their clothes and arms and learned that the barge remained stranded where it landed. Now all five barges had been accounted for.

CHAPTER 32:
Our Escape

THE SECOND DAY after our juncture with the Anagados [i.e., on 22 September 1534], we commended ourselves to God our Lord and made our break. Although the season was late and the prickly pears nearly gone, we still hoped to travel a long distance on acorns which we might find in the woods.

Hurrying along that day in dread of being overtaken, we spied some smoke billows and headed in their direction. We reached them after vespers, to find one Indian. He fled when he saw us coming. We sent the Negro after him, and the Indian stopped when he saw only a lone pursuer. The Negro told him we were seeking the people who made those fires. He said their houses were nearby and he would guide us. We followed as he ran on to announce us.

We saw the houses at sunset. Two crossbow shots before reaching them, we found four Indians waiting to welcome us. We said in Mariame that we were looking for them. They appeared pleased with our presence and took us to their dwellings, where they lodged Dorantes and the Negro in the house of one medicine-man, and Castillo and me in that of another.

These people speak a different language and call themselves Avavares [also spelled Chavavares farther on]. They are the ones who carried bows to the Mariames and, although different in nation and tongue, understand Mariame. They had arrived that day, with their lodges, where we found them [on the upper Medina or Guadalupe River]. Right away they brought us a lot of prickly pears [prickly pears maturing progressively later westward],

84

having heard of us and the wonders our Lord worked by us. If there had been nothing but these cures, they were enough to open ways for us through a poor region like this, find us guides for often uninhabited wastes, and lead us through immediate dangers, not letting us be killed, sustaining us through great want, and instilling in those nations the heart of kindness, as we shall see.

CHAPTER 33:
Our Success with Some of the Afflicted
and My Narrow Escape .

THE VERY EVENING of our arrival, some Indians came to Castillo begging him to cure them of terrible headaches. When he had made the sign of the cross over them and commended them to God, they instantly said that all pain had vanished and went to their houses to get us prickly pears and chunks of venison, something we had tasted of precious little.

We returned many thanks to God, Whose compassion and gifts day by day increased. After the sick had been tended, the Indians danced and sang in festivity till sunrise. The celebration of our coming extended to three days.

When it ended, we inquired of the region farther on, of its people and subsistence. Prickly pears were plentiful throughout, they answered, but this season's had all been gathered by now and the tribes returned home. We would find the country very cold and skins scarce. Reflecting on this, and winter being already upon us, we concluded to stay with these Indians till spring.

Five days after our arrival, the tribe took us with them to gather more prickly pears, at a place where other peoples of different tongues converged. There being no fruit of any kind along the way, we walked five days in gnawing hunger, to a river [the Colorado], where we put up our houses and then went to look for the pods which grow on certain trees [mesquite].

The awkwardness of picking one's way in this vicinity of no paths slowed my own rounds and when, after dark, I went to join the others, who had returned to camp, I got lost. Thank God I found a burning tree, by the warmth of which I passed that cold night.

In the morning I loaded up with sticks and continued my search, carrying two burning brands. For five days I wandered in this way with my fire and my load; otherwise, had my wood failed me where none could be found, I would have lost my kindling fire by the time I located sticks elsewhere. This was all the protection I had against cold, as I wended my way naked as the day I was born.

I would go into the low woods by the river before sunset to prepare myself for the night. First I hollowed out a hole in the ground and threw in fuel, of which there was plenty from the fallen, dry trees in the woods. Then I built four fires around the hole in the form of a cross, and slept in this hole with my fuel supply, covering myself with bundles of the coarse grass which grows thick in those parts. Thus I managed shelter from the cold of night.

One night, the fire fell on the straw as I slept, and blazed so suddenly that it singed my hair in spite of my haste to get out. All this while, I tasted not a mouthful nor found anything to eat. My bare feet bled. By the mercy of God, the wind did not blow from the north in the whole time or I would have died.

At the end of the fifth day I reached the river bank where the Indians were then camped. [The camp seems to have advanced daily.] They and the Christians had given me up for dead, supposing I had been bitten by a snake. Everybody rejoiced to see me; my companions said it had been their great struggle with hunger that kept them from looking for me. All shared prickly pears with me that night, and the next morning we set out for a place where they still abounded. When we got there, we satisfied our great craving, and the Christians gave thanks to the Lord.

[Hallenbeck re-enacted Cabeza de Vaca's five-day adventure one October and reconstructs that he got lost on the Llano and made his bed on successive nights beside the Pedernales, tributaries of the Llano, the San Saber, the north fork of the San Saber, and tributaries of the last two.]

CHAPTER 34:
More Cures

A CROWD OF Indians came to Castillo next morning bringing five sick persons who had cramps. Each of the five offered his bow and arrows, and Castillo accepted them. At sunset [after all-day treatment, or postponing treatment to evening?] he blessed them and commended them to God our Lord. We all prayed the best we could for their health; we knew that only through Him would these people help us so we might emerge from this unhappy existence. And He bestowed health so bountifully that every patient got up the morning following as sound and strong as if he had never had an illness.

This caused great admiration and moved us to further gratitude to our Lord, Whose demonstrated mercy gave us a conviction that He would liberate us and bring us to a place where we might serve Him. I can say for myself that I had always trusted His providence and that He would lead me out of my captivity; I constantly expressed this to my companions.

The Indians having gone with their restored friends, we went over to some thickets where other tribesmen were eating prickly pears. These Indians were Cultalchulches and Malicones, who speak a different dialect. Adjoining them and opposite us were Coayos and Susolas and, on another side, Atayos, who were at war with the Susolas, daily exchanging arrow shots.

Since the Indians all through the region talked only of the wonders which God our Lord worked through us, individuals sought us from many parts in hopes of healing. The evening of the second day after our arrival at these thickets, some of the Susolas came to us and pressed Castillo to go treat their ailing kinsmen—one wounded, the others sick and, among them, a fellow very near his end. Castillo happened to be a timid practitioner—the more so, the more serious and dangerous the case—feeling that his sins would weigh and some day impede his performing cures. The Indians urged me to go heal them. They liked me, remembering I had ministered to them in the grove where they gave us nuts and skins when I first reunited with the Christians [meaning, apparently, on the Island of Doom].

So I had to go with them. Dorantes brought Estevánico and accompanied me. As we drew near the huts of the afflicted, I saw that the man we hoped to save was dead: many mourners were weeping around him, and his house was already down [to be burned with the deceased's possessions]—sure signs that the inhabitant was no more. I found his eyes rolled up, his pulse gone, and every appearance of death, as Dorantes agreed. Taking off the mat that covered him, I supplicated our Lord in his behalf and in behalf of the rest who ailed, as fervently as I could. After my blessing and breathing on him many times, they brought me his bow and a basket of pounded prickly pears.

The [local] natives then took me to treat many others, who had fallen into a stupor, and gave me two more baskets of prickly pears. I, in turn, gave these to the [Susola] Indians who accompanied us. We returned to our lodgings, while the Indians whom we had given the fruit waited till evening to return.

When they got back that evening, they brought the tidings that the "dead" man I had treated had got up whole and walked; he had eaten and spoken with these Sosulas, who further reported that all I had ministered to had recovered and were glad. Throughout the land the effect was a profound wonder and fear. People talked of nothing else, and wherever the fame of it reached, people set out to find us so we should cure them and bless their children.

When the Cultalchulches, who were in company with our [Avavare] Indians, were ready to return to their own heath, they left us all the prickly pears they had, without keeping one. They also gave us valuable cutting flints a palm and a half long, and begged us to remember them and pray to God that they might always be well. We promised. They departed the most contented beings in the world, having given us the best of all they had.

We lived with the Avavares eight months, reckoned by moons, during all which time people came seeking us from many parts and telling us we truly were children of the sun. Up to now, Dorantes and his Negro had not attempted to practice; but under the soliciting pressure of these pilgrims from diverse places, we all became physicians, of whom I was the boldest and most venturous in trying to cure anything. With no exceptions, every patient told us he had been made well. Confidence in our ministrations as infallible extended to a belief that none could die while we remained among them.

CHAPTER 35:
The Story of the Visitation of Mr. Badthing

THE AVAVARES and the tribes we had left behind related an extraordinary experience which, in our equivalent of their vague way of counting, seemed to have occurred fifteen or sixteen years before.

They said that a little man wandered through the region whom they called Badthing [*Mala Cosa*]. He had a beard and they never saw his features distinctly. When he came to a house, the inhabitants trembled and their hair stood on end. A blazing brand would suddenly shine at the door as he rushed in and seized whom he chose, deeply gashing him in the side with a very sharp flint two palms long and a hand wide. He would thrust his hand through the gashes, draw out the entrails, cut a palm's length from one, and throw it on the embers. Then he would gash an arm three times, the second cut on the inside of the. elbow, and would sever the limb. A little later he would begin to rejoin it, and the touch of his hands would instantly heal the wounds.

They said that frequently during the dance he appeared in their midst, sometimes in the dress of a woman, at other times in that of a man. When he liked, he would take a *buhío* up into the air and come crashing down with it. They said they offered him victuals many times but he never ate. They asked him where he came from and where his home was. He pointed to a crevice in the ground and said his home was there below.

We laughed and scoffed. Indignant at our disbelief, they brought us many whom they said had been so seized, and we saw the gash marks in the right places [self-inflicted?]. We told them he was an evil one and, as best we could, taught them that if they would believe in God our Lord and become Christians like us, they need never fear him, nor would he dare come and inflict those wounds; they could be certain he would not appear while we remained in the land. This delighted them and they lost much of their dread.

The same Indians told us they had seen the Asturian and Figueroa with people farther along the coast, whom we designated "those of the figs." [What Cabeza de Vaca knew of the latter, whom he mentions one other time, he must have learned from the Avavares and possibly Castillo and Dorantes (who had more extensive experience of the coast), but he could have encountered some of them in the prickly pear thickets. By "fig," as Hallenbeck suggests, he could well have meant the fruit of the "strawberry cactus" or *pitaya* (*Echinocercus*), some of which he surely ate in that region.]

CHAPTER 36:
Our Life among the Avavares and Arbadaos

ALL THE INDIANS of this region are ignorant of time, either by the sun or moon; nor do they reckon by the month or year. They understand the seasons in terms of the ripening of fruits, the dying of fish, and the position of stars, in which dating they are adept.

The Avavares always treated us well. We lived as free agents, dug our own food, and lugged our loads of wood and water. The houses and our diet were like those of the nation we had just come from, but the Avavares suffer yet greater want, having no corn, acorns, or pecans. We always went naked like them and covered ourselves at night with deerskins.

Six of the eight months we dwelled with these people we endured acute hunger; for fish are not found where they are either. At the end of the eight months, when the prickly pears were just beginning to ripen again [mid-June 1535], I traveled with the Negro—unknown to our hosts —to others a day's journey farther on [up the Colorado]: the Maliacones. When three days had passed, I sent Estevánico to fetch Castillo and Dorantes.

When they got there, the four of us set out with the Maliacones, who were going to find the small fruit of certain trees [red berries of algaritá shrubs, or possibly persimmons?] which they subsist on for ten or twelve days while the prickly pears are maturing. They joined another tribe, the Arbadaos, who astonished us by their weak, emaciated, swollen condition.

We told the Maliacones with whom we had come that we wanted to stop with these Arbadaos. The Maliacones despondently returned the way they came, leaving us alone in the brushland near the Arbadao houses. The observing Arbadaos talked among themselves and came up to us in a body. Four of them took each of us by the hand and led us to their dwellings.

Among them we underwent fiercer hunger than among the Avavares. We ate not more than two handfuls of prickly pears a day, and they were still so green and milky they burned our mouths. In our lack of water, eating brought great thirst. At nearly the end of our endurance we bought two dogs for some nets, with other things, and a skin I used for cover.

I have already said that we went naked through all this country; not being accustomed to going so, we shed our skins twice a year like snakes. The sun and air raised great, painful sores on our chests and shoulders, and our heavy loads caused the cords to cut our arms. The region [the Texas "hill country"] is so broken [with canyons] and so overgrown [with chaparral and mesquite] that often, when we gathered wood, blood flowed from us in many places where the thorns and shrubs tore our flesh. At times, when my turn came to get wood and I had collected it at heavy cost in blood, I could neither drag nor bear it out. My only solace in these labors was to think of the sufferings of our Redeemer, Jesus Christ, and the blood He shed for me. How much worse must have been his torment from the thorns than mine here!

I bartered with these Indians in combs I made for them and in bows, arrows, and nets. We made mats, which are what their houses consist of and for which they feel a keen necessity. Although they know how to make them, they prefer to devote their full time to finding food; when they do not, they get too pinched with hunger.

Some days the Indians would set me to scraping and

softening skins. These were my days of greatest prosperity in that place. I would scrape thoroughly enough to sustain myself two or three days on the scraps. When it happened that these or any people we had left behind gave us a piece of meat, we ate it raw. Had we put it to roast, the first native who came along would have filched it. Not only did we think it better not to risk this, we were in such a condition that roasted meat would have given us pain. We could digest it more easily raw.

Such was our life there, where we earned our meager subsistence by trade in items which were the work of our own hands.

CHAPTER 37:
Our Pushing On

EATING THE DOGS seemed to give us strength enough to go forward; so commending ourselves to the guidance of God our Lord, we took leave of our hosts, who pointed out the way to others nearby who spoke their language.

Rain caught us. We traveled the day in the wet and got lost. At last, we made for an extensive scrub wood stretch, where we stopped and pulled prickly pear pads, which we cooked overnight in a hot oven we made. By morning they were ready. [Hallenbeck thinks the Spaniards had come close to the confluence of the Concho and Colorado or, possibly, a little above it.]

After eating, we put ourselves again in the hands of God and set forth. We located the path we had lost and, after passing another scrub wood stretch, saw houses. Two women who were walking in the "forest" with some boys fled deep into it in fright to call their men, when they noticed us heading for the houses. The men arrived and hid behind trees to look at us. We called to them, and they came up very timidly. After some conversation, they told us their food was very scarce and that many houses of their people stood close by, to which they would conduct us.

At nightfall we came to a village of fifty dwellings. The residents looked at us in astonishment and fear. When they grew somewhat accustomed to our appearance, they felt our faces and bodies and then their own, comparing. [The Spaniards' beards and hairy chests and legs probably occasioned the perplexity.]

We stayed in that place overnight. In the morning the Indians brought us their sick, beseeching our blessing. They shared with us what they had to eat—prickly pear pads and the green fruit roasted. Because they did this with kindness and good will, gladly foregoing food to give us some, we tarried here several days.

Other Indians came from beyond in that interval and, when they were about to depart, we told our hosts we wanted to go with them. Our hosts felt quite uneasy at this and pressed us warmly to stay. In the midst of their weeping we left them.

CHAPTER 38:
Customs of that Region

FROM THE ISLAND of Doom to this land, all the Indians we saw have the custom of not sleeping with their wives from the time they are discovered pregnant to two years after giving birth. Children are suckled until they are twelve, when they are old enough to find their own support. We asked why they thus prolonged the nursing period, and they said that the poverty of the land frequently meant—as we witnessed—going two or three days without eating, sometimes four; if children were not allowed to suckle in seasons of scarcity, those who did not famish would be weaklings.

Anyone who chances to fall sick on a foraging trip and cannot keep up with the rest is left to die, unless he be a son or brother; him they will help, even to carrying on their back.

It is common among them all to leave their wives when there is disagreement, and directly reconnect with whomever they please. This is the course of men who are childless. Those who have children never abandon their wives.

When Indian men get into an argument in their villages, they fist-fight until exhausted, then separate. Sometimes the women will go between and part them, but men never interfere. No matter what the disaffection, they do not resort to bows and arrows. After a fight, the disputants take their houses (and families) and go live apart from each other in the scrub wood until they have cooled off; then they return and from that moment are friends as if nothing had happened. No intermediary is needed to mend their friendship.

In case the quarrelers are single men, they repair to some neighboring people (instead of the scrub wood), who, even if enemies, welcome them warmly and give so largely of what they have that when the quarrelers' animosity subsides, they return to their home village rich.

CHAPTER 39:
Indian Warfare

ALL THESE [plains] tribes are warlike, and have as much strategy for protection against enemies as if they had been reared in Italy in continual feuds. When in a part of the country where enemies might attack, they place their houses on the skirt of a scrub wood "forest," the thickest and most tangled they can find, and dig a ditch in which they sleep. The warriors cover themselves with small brush, leaving loopholes, and are so camouflaged that, if come upon, they are not discovered.

They open a very narrow pathway into the interior of the scrub stand, where a spot is prepared for the women and children to sleep. At nightfall they kindle fires in their lodges to make possible spies think the tribe is inside them. Before daybreak they relight these fires. Should an enemy come to assault the lodges, the defenders in the ditch sally out and inflict much injury before they are seen or located. When no timber presents itself for this kind of shelter and ambush overnight, they arrange themselves on selected open ground and invest it with trenches covered with brush, spacing apertures to shoot arrows through.

Once while I was with the Aguenes [Doguenes], their [Quevene] enemies fell upon them suddenly at midnight, killed three, and wounded many. The Aguenes ran from their houses into the fields facing. When they perceived their assailants had retired, they went back to pick up all the arrows the latter had shot and followed after them so stealthily that the aggressors did not suspect their arrival in the village that night. At 4 A.M. the Aguenes attacked, killed five, and wounded quite a few. The Quevenes fled from their houses, leaving their bows and all they owned behind. In a little while, the wives of the Quevene warriors came to the Aguenes and made a treaty of friendship. The women, on the other hand, sometimes are the cause of war.

All these nations, when they have personal enmities and are not related, assassinate at night, waylay, and inflict gross atrocities on each other.

They are the most vigilant in danger of any people I ever knew. If they fear an enemy, they stay awake all night, each warrior with a bow and a dozen arrows at his side. If one inclines to doze, he tests his bow and gives the string a twist if it is not taut enough.

Warriors often issue from their houses bending to the

ground so they cannot be seen, peering all around to catch every object. If they detect anything suspicious, they at once are in the bushes with their bows and arrows, and remain there all day, running from place to place—where they think they need to be or where they think the enemy lurks. With daylight they unbend their bows until they go out to hunt. The strings are deer sinews.

The way they battle is to bend low to the ground, constantly speaking [yelling], and leap from one point to another, avoiding the shafts shot at them. Their maneuvering is so effective that a crossbow or musket does them little damage; they rather scorn them, especially when they can move nimbly about on an open field. Our weapons are, however, good for defiles and in water. Everywhere else, the horse will best subdue, being what the natives universally dread [to generalize from Spanish experience in Florida, Mexico, and the West Indies].

Whoever fights them must show no fear and no desire for anything that is theirs. While a war is on, they must be treated with utmost rigor; for if they detect the slightest timidity or covetousness, they are a race who readily note and exploit opportunities for vengeance. They draw strength from any weakness in their adversaries.

When they exhaust their supply of arrows in battle, each side withdraws his own way, neither following the other even if preponderant, such being their custom. At times an Indian will be run through by an arrow; but if it does not hit the entrails or heart, he recovers.

I believe these people see and hear better and have keener senses in general than any in the world. They know great hunger, thirst, and cold, as if they were made for enduring these more than other men, by habit and nature.

I have wanted to say this much, not merely to indulge the curiosity of humans about each other, but to impart a knowledge of usages and artifices which would be of value to those who might sometime in the future find themselves among these people.

CHAPTER 40:
An Enumeration of the Nations and Tongues

I SHOULD LIKE TO catalog the natives and their languages all the way from the Island of Doom to the farthest Cuchendados.

Two languages are found on the island: those spoken by the Capoques and Han.

On the mainland over against the island are the Charruco, who take their name from the forests where they live.

Advancing along the coast, we come to the Deguenes and, opposite them, the Mendica. Farther down the coast are the Quevenes and, behind them inland, the Mariames. Continuing by the coast: the Guaycones and, behind them inland, the Yeguaces.

After these come the Atayos, in their rear the Decubadaos, and beyond them many others in the same direction.

By the coast live the Quitoles and, just behind them inland, the Chavavares and, adjoining them in order: the Maliacones, Cultalchulches, Susolas, and Comos. By the coast farther on are the Camolas and, on the same coast beyond them, those we called the "Fig People." [Some tribes are listed that are not mentioned elsewhere, and some that are mentioned elsewhere are not listed.]

They all differ in their habitations, villages, and tongues. In one language, "Look here" is *Arre aca* when addressing a person, and *So* when addressing a dog. [Cabeza de Vaca seems to have intended a discussion of dialects but failed to follow through.]

CHAPTER 41:
A Smoke; a Tea; Women and Eunuchs

EVERYWHERE they produce a stupor with a smoke [of, presumably, *peyote* cactus, imported from tribes of the Río Grande valley and southward], for which they will give whatever they possess.

They drink a yellow tea made of leaves from a holly-like shrub [*Ilex cassine*] which they parch in a pot; then the pot is filled with water while still on the fire. [This became popularly known elsewhere as "black drink" and "Carolina tea."] When the beverage has boiled twice, they pour it into a jar and thence into a half gourd. As soon as it is frothy, they drink it as hot as they can stand. From the time it is poured from the pot to the time of the first sip, they are shouting, "Who wants to drink?"

When the women hear these shouts, they stand motionless, fearing to move. Even if heavily laden, they dare not budge. Should a woman make a motion, they dishonor her, beat her with sticks, and in great vexation throw out the liquor that is prepared. Those who have drunk any of it regurgitate, which they do readily and painlessly. They say they do this because a woman's movement when she hears the shout causes the tea to carry something pernicious into the drinker's body which will presently kill him.

At the time of boiling, the pot must be covered. If it happens to be open when a woman passes, the rest of that potful is thrown out. The village is three days drinking this tea, eating nothing the whole time. Each person has an arroba and a half [about five or six gallons] a day.

When the women have their indisposition, they seek food only for themselves; no one else will eat of what they bring.

99

In the time I was among these people, I witnessed a diabolical practice: a man living with a eunuch. Eunuchs go partly dressed, like women, and perform women's duties, but use the bow and carry very heavy loads. We saw many thus mutilated. They are more muscular and taller than other men and can lift tremendous weight.

CHAPTER 42:
Four Fresh Receptions

AFTER PARTING from our weeping hosts, we went with the others, who had come to visit, and were hospitably received in the latters' houses. They brought their children to us to touch their heads and gave us a great quantity of mesquite bean flour.

The mesquite bean, while hanging on the tree, is very bitter like the carob bean but, when mixed with earth, is sweet and wholesome. The Indian method of preparing it is to dig a fairly deep hole in the ground, throw in the beans, and pound them with a club the thickness of a leg and a fathom and a half long, until they are well mashed. Besides the earth that gets mixed in from the bottom and sides of the hole, the Indians add some handfuls, then pound awhile longer. They throw the meal into a basket-like jar and pour water on it until it is covered. The pounder tastes it. If he thinks it not sweet enough, he calls for more earth to stir in, which is added until he judges the dish just right.

Then all squat round, and each takes out as much as he can with one hand. The pits and hulls are thrown onto a hide; the pounder puts them back into the "jar," where more water is poured on; and again the pits and hulls are salvaged. This process is repeated three or four times per pounding. To the partakers, the dish is a great banquet. Their stomachs grow grossly distended from the quantity of earth and water they swallow. Because of us, our newly adopted hosts made an extended festival of this sort, together with big *areitos* in the time we tarried with them. At night, during this celebration, the tribe assigned twenty-four Indian men to stand sentry before the lodge we slept in to bar entrance [and exit?] to any until sunrise.

When we proposed to leave this tribe, some women of another who lived farther on came to visit. They told us the whereabouts of their village, and we set out for it, although our hosts begged us to stay at least that day—the neighboring village was distant; no path led there; the women had arrived tired and would go with us as guides on the morrow refreshed. We left anyway.

Soon afterward, some of the visiting women plus some women of the village they were visiting followed us. There being no paths in that vicinity, we presently got lost and traveled so four leagues when, stopping at a spring [Big Spring, Texas], we found the pursuing women already there ahead of us. They told us what exertion they had made to overtake us. [Hallenbeck thinks the women followed a trail that did exist, along the Colorado, but that the Spaniards attempted a shortcut to the Concho. Two trails intersected at Big Spring, just south of the present city named after it.]

We went on, taking the women for guides, and towards evening forded a chest-deep river [the Concho]. It had a swift current and [swelled by August rains,] may have been as wide as the one in Seville [the Guadalquivir, which is about a hundred paces across].

At sunset we reached a village of a hundred huts. All the people who lived in them were awaiting us at the village outskirts with terrific yelling and violent slapping of their hands against their thighs. They had with them their precious perforated gourd rattles (pebbles inside) which they produce only at such important occasions as the dance or a medical ceremony and which no one but the owner dares touch. They say there is a virtue in them and that, since they do not grow in that area, they obviously come from heaven. All they know is that the rivers bring them when they flood. [The rivers would have been the Pecos and Río Grande, which occasionally washed gourds down from the bottomland plots far above, where the pueblo Indians grew them. The Concho Indians must have acquired the salvaged floaters by trade.]

This people hysterically crowded upon us, everyone competing to touch us first; we were· nearly killed in the crush. Without letting our feet touch ground, they carried us to the huts they had made for us. We took refuge in them and absolutely refused to be feasted that night. They themselves, however, sang and danced the whole night through. In the morning they brought every single inhabitant of the village for us to touch and bless as they had heard we had done elsewhere. After our performance, they presented many arrows to the women of the other village who had accompanied theirs.

When we left next day, all the people of the place went with us, and the next people received us as well as the last, giving us of what they had to eat, including the deer they had killed that day. Here we saw a new custom. Members of the tribe would take the bows and arrows, shoes and beads (if they wore any) from individuals who came to get cured and lay them before us as inducement. As soon as the sick were treated, they went away glad, saying they were sound.

We left these Indians and went on to others, who also welcomed us and brought us their sick who, when blessed, declared themselves sound. If anyone did not actually recover, he still contended he would. What they who did recover related caused general rejoicing and dancing; so we got no sleep.

CHAPTER 43:
A Strange New Development

LEAVING THESE INDIANS, we proceeded to the next village, where another novel custom commenced: Those who accompanied us plundered our hospitable new hosts and ransacked their huts, leaving nothing. We watched this with deep concern but were in no position to do anything about it; so for the present had to bear with it until such time as we might gain greater authority. Those who had lost their possessions, seeing our dejection, tried to console us. They said they were so honored to have us that their property was well bestowed—and that they would get repaid by others farther on, who were very rich.

All through the day's travel we had been badly hampered by the hordes of Indians following us. We could not have escaped if we had tried, they pursued so closely just to touch us. Their insistence on this privilege cost us three hours in going through them so they might depart. Next day, all the inhabitants of the newly reached village came before us. The majority had one clouded eye and others were completely blind, to our astonishment. They are a people of fine forms, pleasant features, and whiter than any of the nations we had so far seen.

Here we began to see mountains. They seemed to sweep in succession from the North Sea and, from what the Indians told us, we believe they rise fifteen leagues from the sea. [The mountains which came in view on the high plains between the Concho and the Pecos were the Davis, Lower Guadalupe, and Upper Guadalupe ranges, which sweep toward the Gulf, which in the 16th century was referred to as the North Sea; it was anyway an extension of the Atlantic, which was the North Sea to Balboa on the

Isthmus of Panama, in relation to the Pacific, or South Sea. Cabeza de Vaca may have meant "toward" when he said "from"; he may even have viewed them as sweeping northward; or he may have believed, like many later explorers, that a sea lay a short distance north in the middle of the continent.]

We headed towards these mountains, with our newest hosts, who were willing to guide us by way of a related settlement but by no means to risk letting their enemies get in on this great good which they thought we represented. They plundered their relatives as though they were enemies when we arrived, but the people there knew the custom and had hidden some things which, after welcoming us with a festive demonstration, they brought out and presented us: beads, ochre, and some little bags of mica. Following custom, we handed them over to the plundering Indians who came with us, who thereupon resumed their dances and festivities and sent to a nearby village so their relatives there could come see us.

The latter showed up that afternoon, bringing us beads, bows, and other trifles, which we also distributed. As we were about to get on next morning, the local villagers all wanted to take us to friends of theirs who lived at the top of the ridge; many houses stood there and the residents would give us various things, they said. But it was out of our way and we decided to continue our course on the same trail along the plain toward the mountains, which we believed close to the coast where people are mean. Having found the people of the interior better off and milder toward us, we preferred to bear inland. We also felt surer of finding the interior more populous and more amply provisioned. [The Spaniards evidently thought they had been traveling roughly parallel to the coast and veered northwestward in order to keep clear of such people as had enslaved them. As Hallenbeck points out, Pineda's map could have misled them because it puts Matagorda Bay where the Mississippi ought to be.] We further chose this 'course to find out more about the country so that, should God our Lord please to lead any of us to the land of

Christians, we might carry information of it with us. [The reason that continuing along the same trail would be to veer "inland" is that here it ran into and along the Pecos River.]

When the Indians saw our determination to keep to this course, they warned us that we would find nobody, nor prickly pears or anything else to eat, and begged us to delay at least that day; so we did. They promptly sent two of their number to seek people along the trail ahead. We left next morning, taking several Indians with us. The women carried water [for the saline Pecos is undrinkable], and such was our authority that none dared drink but by our leave.

Two leagues out, we met those who had scouted ahead. They said they had found no one; which news seemed to dishearten our escort, who again pleaded with us to go by way of the mountains. When they saw we would not be swayed, they regretfully left us and returned down the river to their huts, while we ascended alongside it.

Not long afterward we came upon two women bearing burdens, which they set down when they saw us and offered some of what they carried. It was cornmeal! [Doubtless it was an item of commerce originating among pueblo Indians 250 or 300 miles distant; though it is possible that some of these semi-migrant plains Indians cultivated small corn plots the Spaniards never saw.] They told us that farther up that river we would find not only dwellings but plenty of prickly pears and meal. We bade them *adiós;* they were on their way to those we had just left.

We walked till sunset, when we reached a *ranchería* [or temporary encampment, as Hallenbeck defines it] of some twenty houses. The inhabitants received us with weeping and grieving; for they knew that wherever we came would be plundered by those escorting us. When they saw we were unescorted, they got over their apprehension and gave us prickly pears, though nothing more. We stayed overnight.

At dawn, the Indians we had left the day before surprised our latest hosts who, having neglected to conceal anything, lost all they had and shed copious tears. Their plunderers told them in consolation that we were children of the sun with power to save or destroy, along with even bigger lies, which none can tell better than they. They cautioned our hosts to avoid offending us in any way, to give us all they had [left], and to take us to a populous village which custom privileged them to pillage. Then the plunderers went back.

Taking good heed, our new hosts began to treat us with the same awe and deference the others had shown. We traveled with them three days to a large settlement. Before we got there, our escort transmitted to the residents what they had recently heard, with much embroidery; for these people are fond of romance and make great liars, especially where they have a vested interest.

As we approached the houses, therefore, the residents rushed out to receive us royally. Among other articles, two of their medicine-men gave us two gourds, which we ever after carried with us, to the enhancement of the Indians' reverence of us. Our escort duly sacked the houses but, being few and their victims many, they had to abandon more than half of what they took as more than they could carry.

CHAPTER 44:

Rabbit Hunts and Processions of Thousands

WE TRAVELED in that region through so many different villages of such diverse tongues that my memory gets confused. They ever plundered each other, and those who lost were as content as those who gained. We attracted more followers than we could employ or manage.

As we went through these valleys, every Indian carried a club three palms long and kept alert. When a rabbit jumped (the country teems with these animals), they quickly surrounded him and threw their clubs with amazing accuracy, driving him from one man to another. I cannot imagine a sport that is more fun, as often the rabbit runs right into your hand. By the time we stopped for the night, the Indians had provided us with eight or ten backloads of rabbits apiece.

The archers, instead of staying with us, deployed in the mountains after deer and came back at dark with five or six for each of us, besides quail and other game. Whatever the Indians killed or found, they brought before us, not daring to eat anything until we had blessed it, even if they were desperately hungry. They themselves had established this rule when they took up their march with us.

The women brought many mats, of which the men made us houses—a separate one for each of us together with his personal attendants. When these were put up, we ordered the deer and hares roasted, and the rest of what had been taken. They did this efficiently in ovens they constructed for the purpose. We took a little from each ovenload and gave the rest to the principal personage of our procession to divide among his people. Every Indian brought his portion to us to be breathed on and blessed before he would dare touch it. When you consider that we were frequently accompanied by three or four thousand Indians and were obliged to sanctify the food and drink of each one, as well as grant permission for the many things they asked to do, you can appreciate our inconvenience. The women would bring us prickly pears, spiders, worms—whatever they might gather—strictly foregoing even these until we had made the sign of the cross over them, though the women might have been starving at the time.

Our enormous escort still with us, we crossed a large river which flowed from the north [the Pecos, the second day after the Spaniards first saw the mountains; for Cabeza de Vaca, admittedly confused in his recollections in this

section, is resummarizing the segment of the trip he has
already traced. In both editions of his narrative, in fact,
this reminiscence comes after the crossing of the mountains, but is here transposed back to its proper place. The
sentence interrupted reviews the sequence where the Indians urged taking the mountain route but the Spaniards
kept on up the Pecos.]; we then traversed thirty leagues
of plains, to be met by a throng who had come a long way
to give us a reception on the trail comparable to the ones
we had been receiving in the villages and *rancherías* lately.
They accompanied us on to their dwellings.

CHAPTER 45:
My Famous Operation in the
Mountain Country

FROM HERE [on the Pecos in the vicinity of Carlsbad, New
Mexico] we went along the base of the mountains [via
the Río Peñasco and then the Elk Creek fork], striking
inland [northwestward] more than fifty leagues, at the end
of which we came upon forty or so houses.

Among the things the people there gave us was a big
copper rattle which they presented Andrés Dorantes. It
had a face represented on it and the natives prized it
highly. They told Dorantes they had received it from
their neighbors. Where did *they* get it? It had been brought
from the north, where there was a lot of it, replied the
natives, who considered copper very valuable. Wherever
it came from, we concluded the place must have a foundry
to have cast the copper in hollow form. [Hallenbeck calls
attention to five such rattles excavated at a prehistoric
'*ranchería* about thirty miles north of the approximate
site of the gift to Dorantes. To Hallenbeck they suggested

primitive sleigh bells; each had one pebble inside. Shells from the Pacific coast and turquoises from northern New Mexico were found with the copper rattles.]

Departing next morning [up Elk Creek], we went over a mountain seven leagues in magnitude [a close estimate; Hallenbeck measured the distance by this route over the 6,500-foot pass in the Sacramento range at seventeen miles from noticeable beginning of the ascent to noticeable end of the descent]. Its stones are iron slags. [What Cabeza de Vaca mistook for iron slag could have been iron ore, igneous rock, or honeycombed limestone, says Hallenbeck.]

At night we came to many dwellings seated on the banks of a very beautiful stream [the Río Tularosa. When the Spaniards went over the summit of the mountain ridge, they passed from the head of Elk Creek to the head of the Río Tularosa and followed the latter river down.] The residents came halfway out on the trail to greet us, bringing their children on their backs. They gave us many little bags of mica [again "silver" in the 1542 edition and "pearl" in the 1555] and powdered lead [or antimony or manganese] which they smear on their faces [for a dark blue war paint]; many beads and cowhide [i.e., buffalo skin] blankets—loading all who attended us with everything they had.

They eat prickly pears and pine nuts; for small pine trees [the piñon (*Pinus edulis*)] grow in that region [thick and extensively in those mountains, the *Joint Report* adds] with egg-shaped cones whose nuts are better than those of Castile because of their thin husks. The nuts are beaten into balls while still green and so eaten; if the nuts are dry, they are pounded with the husks and consumed as meal. [The *Joint Report* says the Indians here wore cotton shawls which they said came from the north across the land from the South Sea. Thus by trade they had acquired blankets from the pueblo Indians to the north, who in turn acquired them from the Moqui to the west.] Once our new hosts touched us, they ran back and forth bringing us all kinds of items from their houses for our journey.

They fetched me a man who, they said, had long since been shot in the shoulder through the back and that the arrowhead had lodged above his heart. He said it was very painful and kept him sick. I probed the wound and discovered the arrowhead had passed through the cartilage. With a flint knife I opened the fellow's chest until I could see that the point was sideways and would be difficult to extract. But I cut on and, at last, inserting my knife-point deep, was able to work the arrowhead·out with great effort. It was huge. With a deer bone, I further demonstrated my surgical skill with two stitches while blood drenched me, and stanched the flow with hair from a hide. The villagers asked me for the arrowhead, which I gave them. The whole population came to look at it, and they sent it into the back country so the people there could see it.

They celebrated this operation with their customary dances and festivities. Next day, I cut the stitches and the patient was well. My incision appeared only like a crease in the palm of the hand. He said he felt no pain or sensitivity there at all.

Now this cure so inflated our fame all over the region that we could control whatever the inhabitants cherished.

We showed them the copper rattle we had recently been given, and they told us that many layers of this material were buried in the place whence it came, that this [metal] was·highly valued, and that the people who made it lived in fixed dwellings. We conceived the country they spoke of to be on the South Sea, which we had always understood was richer in mineral resources than that of the North.

CHAPTER 46:
The Severe Month's March to the Great River

FROM HERE the manner of receiving. us changed, in that those who came out to greet us with presents did not get despoiled or their houses rifled; rather, when we got to their houses, they themselves offered us everything they had, including the houses, and we turned the things over to the chief personages in our escort to distribute. The people who had relinquished their property always, of course, followed us to the next large village to recoup. They would warn the villagers among whom we came to be sure to hold back nothing, since we knew all and could cause them to die; the sun revealed everything to us. For the first few days a new group walked with us they would continually tremble and dared not speak or even look up to the heavens.

They [of the Tularosa village] guided us [down the Tularosa then south] through more than fifty leagues, mostly over rugged mountain desert so dry there was a dearth of game, and we suffered great hunger. [It was necessary to take this hard route over spurs and foothills of the Sacramentos, Hallenbeck points out, because no watering places likely occurred in the flatter country below to the west. As it was, he says, five of the seven watering places along this eighty-mile foothill stretch lay in less accessible places higher up; so that the foothill route amounted to a compromise. Hallenbeck found remains of a *ranchería* at each of the seven watering places. Although it was late fall and the prickly pear season past, the Spaniards and their retinue must have been afforded minimal relief at these stages, from pine nut globs (potholes for pine nut beating can be seen at each of the watering sites) and deer, as well as water. Cabeza de Vaca patently means by "fifty leagues" (150 miles more or less) the total distance the Tularosa Indians escorted the Spaniards, not just the mountainous 80-mile stretch. Hallenbeck measured the trail on through the subsequent plain at a total of 140 or 145 miles, or about 170 with detours to watering places.]

Many of the people began to sicken from the privation and exertion of negotiating those sterile, difficult ridges. Our escort, however, conducted us across a thirty-league plain [between the Sacramentos and the Huecos], and we found many persons come a long distance on the trail to greet us [meaning that heralds had, as usual, hastened ahead of the main party] and welcomed us like those before. They brought double the quantity of goods for our escort that the latter could carry. I told the givers to reclaim what was left so it would not go to waste; but they refused, saying it was not their custom, once they had given something, to take it back; so half the gifts lay where they were to decay.

We told our new hosts that we wished to go where the sun sets; but they said people in that direction were remote. We commanded them to send and make known our coming anyway. They stalled and made various excuses, because the people to the west were their enemies, whom they wanted to avoid. Not daring to disobey, however, they sent two women—one of their own and the other a captive from the "remote" enemy people—for women can deal as neutrals anywhere, even during war. We followed them to a stopping place where we agreed to wait, and waited five days. The Indians who stayed with us concluded the women could not have found anybody.

We told them, then, to conduct us northward. They answered as before: there were no people in that direction for a very long distance, nothing to eat, and no water. When we remained adamant, they still excused themselves as best they could, and our gorge rose. One night I went to sleep in the woods apart from them, but they shortly came to me and stayed awake all night telling me of their terror and pleading with me to be angry no longer, that they would lead us where we would though it meant their death. We still feigned displeasure in order to keep the upper hand, and a singular circumstance strengthened that hand mightily.

That very day, many of the Indians had fallen ill, and the next day eight men died. All over that area, wherever this became known, the natives panicked; they seemed to think they would die at sight of us. They supplicated us to kill no more of them in our wrath, for they believed we caused their death by merely willing it. The truth is, we could hardly have felt more distressed—at their loss and also at the possibility that they would either all die off or abandon us in fright and that other tribes ever after would flee from us. We prayed to God our Lord to restore them and, from that moment, the sick began to mend.

We marveled that the parents, brothers, and wives of those who had died should have shown such sympathy for them in their suffering, but no feeling at all once the sick had died. There was no weeping, no speaking among the bereaved, no gestures, or even advancing to the bodies until we ordered them buried.

While we lived with these people, which was more than half a month, we saw no one converse; we did not even see an infant smile. They took away the only infant who cried and scratched it from the shoulders to the legs with sharp mouse teeth. Horrified, I reprimanded them. They said they were punishing the child for crying in my presence. Such an ironclad fear these people imparted to all who lately came to know us, so the latter would give up to us whatever they owned, the former knowing we kept nothing and would pass it on to them. These were the most obedient people we had found anywhere, also in general the best looking.

Three days had passed since we came to this stopping place, and the sick had recovered. Now the women we had sent out returned [though Cabeza de Vaca earlier had said they did not return for five days]. They said they found few people, nearly all having gone for cattle [buf-

falo], it being the season. [The season, as Hallenbeck
notes, occurred after the first frost, which in those parts
comes around the last of October (Old Style). Before then,
the meat would spoil too quickly. Also, both the meat and
the pelts were best in late November and in December.
Thus this point in the narrative is roughly datable at sometime after October 31 (1535).] We commanded the con-
valescent to remain and the well to continue with us and
that, at the end of two days' travel, the same women must
go on with two of us to fetch those hunters to receive us.
[Families accompanied the men who went out to hunt
buffalo, because it was the women who flayed the victims.]

So next morning the able-bodied set forth with us. At
the end of three *jornadas* [stages between stops (at settlements), thus often far short of a usual day's journey] we
held up while Alonso del Castillo went ahead with Estevánico, the Negro, taking the two women for guides. The
captive one led them to a river [the Río Grande] which ran
between mountains where her father's town lay. The dwellings of this town [just below El Paso] were the first to be
seen which looked like real houses.

After Castillo and Estevánico got there and talked with
the residents, Castillo, with five or six of them, returned at
the end of three days to the spot we had held up. He reported finding permanent houses where the people ate
beans and melons [squash] and that he had seen corn.
Overjoyed at this news, we gave boundless thanks to our
Lord.

Castillo further told us that the Negro was on his way
with the whole population of the town to await us on the
trail not far off. Up we got and, in a league and a half,
met the Negro and the townspeople coming to greet us.
They piled up for us beans, many squashes, gourds for
carrying water, cowhide blankets, etc. As this people were
enemies of the people escorting us—they did not speak
each other's language either—we discharged the latter
after turning over to them what we had just received, and
proceeded with the new hosts.

Six leagues from there, as dusk was falling, we reached the houses, where festive ceremonies welcomed us. We stayed one day, moving on with these Indians the next. They took us to the settlements of others, who lived on the same food.

[These were not pueblo Indians; nor were their towns quite so stationary as they appeared to the Spaniards. It turns out that these Indians did not weave or make pottery, as the truly sedentary pueblo Indians did; and their farm-ing methods forced them to move every so often to find unexhausted soil. What shifts had occurred by the time of various later evidence, we do not know; but after the exhaustive discussions of Sauer and Hallenbeck, the best tentative identification of these buffalo-hunting Indians would be Athapascan Mansos or Jumanos.]

CHAPTER 47:
The Cow People

FROM NOW ON, the natives, when apprised of our approach, did not throng out on the trail to welcome us as hereto-fore, but we found them [in an attitude of extreme dread and supplication] sitting in their houses facing the wall with bowed heads, their hair pulled down over their eyes, and all their possessions piled in the middle of the floor. Houses they had made to accommodate us stood ready. Our gifts, from the first place that received us like this on, included many skin blankets; but there was nothing they owned that they did not freely give us.

They are the best looking people we saw, the strongest and most energetic, and who most readily understood us and answered our questions. We called them the "Cow People," because more cattle are killed in their vicinity than anywhere; for more than fifty leagues up that river they prey on the cows.

They go as absolutely naked as the first Indians we encountered, the women of course wearing deerskins, as well as a few men, mostly those too old to fight anymore. The country is incredibly populous.

We asked how it happened they did not plant corn. So they would not lose what they planted, was the answer: no rain two years in a row; moles got the seed; must have plenty rain before planting again. They begged us to tell the sky to rain; we promised we would pray. Where, we asked them, did they get the corn they had? From where the sun goes down; in that country it grew all over; the quickest way there was that path. They did not wish to go with us, so we asked them to be more explicit. They said to take the path along the river northward; otherwise we would go seventeen *jornadas* without finding anything to eat but *chacan* [juniper "berries" (actually proto-cones)] which, even after ground between stones, is hard to get down, being so woody and pungent—and sure enough, when they showed us a sample we could not eat it. The people who lived along the river route were enemies of the Cow People but spoke the same tongue; though they would have nothing to eat to give, they would nevertheless receive us hospitably and load us with cotton blankets, hides, etc., said our hosts who, however, advised against that route.

[The *Joint Report* clarifies that the Indians said there was corn country both west and north, but even to reach that of the west it was necessary to travel fifteen *jornadas* northward along the river. Hallenbeck points out that the Indians could have been thinking of the ninety-mile desert Journey of Death on the way to the pueblos when they discouraged staying on the northern course once reaching the crossroads ford.]

Uncertain as to the better choice, we tarried another couple of days with these Indians, who plied us with beans and calabashes. Their method of cooking is so novel and strange, let me describe it. Not having discovered pots, they fill a medium-sized calabash hull full of water and drop red-hot rocks in it with stick tongs until the water boils. Then for the whole while that whatever they put in to cook is cooking, they keep transferring more rocks from the fire and taking out the spent ones. They know just which rocks take heat best, and the water boils on and on.

CHAPTER 48:
The Long Swing-Around

AFTER THE TWO DAYS of indecision, we concluded that our destiny lay toward the sunset and so took the trail north only as far as we had to in order to reach the westward one, and then swung down until eventually we came out at the South Sea. The seventeen *jornadas* of hunger the Cow People warned us of, and which proved to be just as bad as they said, could not deter us.

During this desert ascent by the river [the Río Grande, stopping at *rancherías* as usual, according to the *Joint Report*], the [Suma] Indians gave us many cowhides, but we passed up their *chacan* in favor of about a handful of deer tallow a day, which we had long since learned to save for such times of famine.

After seventeen *jornadas* we forded the very wide, chest-deep, southern flowing river [at Rincon, New Mexico] and traveled another seventeen [over twenty, says the *Joint Report* more plausibly]. [Part of the preceding sentence is transposed from the second paragraph of chapter 46 where Cabeza de Vaca makes a glaringly premature reference to the same fording.]

[Hallenbeck traces the Spaniards' trail up the west side of the Río Grande after the Rincon crossing, to Berrenda Creek, up that creek through a gap in the Mimbres Mountains and down the Río Mimbres a few miles, westward up San Vincente Creek (which was probably dry at the time) and across the Burro Mountains via a western tributary of the creek, to the Gila River near Redrock, New Mexico; down the Gila for the remaining twelve or fifteen miles that it flows southwestward, then across country in the same direction through the low Peloncillo Mountains, across the Arizona border to the spring at San Simone; and on—still southwestward—to the pass between the Dos Cabezos and Chiricahua Mountains. The longest stretch without water on this route would have been the lower twelve miles of Berrenda Creek. The *Joint Report* speaks of stopping on occasion, as had long been customary with the Spaniards, and of being provided with rabbits in excess of need; and that this country was somewhat hunger-stricken, though less than that along the Río Grande out of El Paso. The travelers evidently were too jaded to note many remarkable details of the more than 500-mile segment of this chapter. Hallenbeck points out that their silence confirms that they negotiated no very difficult mountain passes or particularly heavy timber, followed no one stream unduly far, trudged over no sand dunes, suffered no desperate thirst, and managed to put up at a *ranchería* every frosty night this early winter.]

One day as the sun went down out on the plains between [the Gila River and the] massive [Chiricahua] mountains, we came upon people who for a third of the year eat nothing but powdered straw [dried desert herbs] and, that being the season we passed through, we had to eat it ourselves until at last, at the end of the seventeen [or twenty-plus] *jornadas,* we got to the [Ópata] people of permanent houses who had plenty of corn.

[After passing between the Dos Cabezos and Chiricahuas, the Spaniards, according to Hallenbeck, came south along the western slopes of the Chiricahuas, where more water was available than on the eastern, as their guides well knew. Toward the terminus of this range, they struck toward the east slope of the Perilla Mountains and thence through a district of many alternative paths and springs to the San Bernardino Valley of northern Sonora, Mexico, where the Ópatas dwelled.]

They gave us a great quantity of corn, cornmeal, calabashes, beans, and cotton blankets, all of which we loaded onto the guides who had led us here, and they went back the happiest people on earth. We gave many thanks to God our Lord for bringing us to this land of abundance.

Some of the houses here are made of earth, the rest of cane mats. We marched more than a hundred leagues [actually about 210 miles, not counting possible detours, down the San Bernardino Valley] through continuously inhabited country of such domiciles, where corn and beans remained plentiful. The people [who, at the end of the hundred leagues, were Pimas] gave us innumerable deerhide and cotton blankets, the latter better than those of New Spain, beads made of coral from the South Sea, fine [and genuine] turquoises from the north—in fact, everything they had, including a special gift to me [1555 edition; to Dorantes (1542 edition)] of five emerald [probably malachite] arrowheads such as they use in their singing and dancing. These looked quite valuable. I asked where they came from. They said from lofty mountains to the north, where there were towns of great population and great houses, and that the arrowheads had been purchased with feather bushes and parrot plumes [doubtless from southern Sonora and possibly farther south].

Among this people, women are better treated than in any part of the Indies we had come through. They wear knee-length cotton shirts and, over them, half-sleeved skirts of scraped deerskin that reach to the ground and that are laced together in front with leather strips. The women soap this outer garment with a certain root [amole, the yucca root] which cleanses well and keeps the deerskin becoming. And they wear shoes.

All the people, sick and well, came to us in an attitude of urgency to be touched and blessed; only with great labor did we get through them all. Speaking of labor, there were many times that women accompanying us gave birth to babies and, as soon as they were born, the mothers would bring them to us for our touch and blessing.

These Indians ever stayed with us until they safely delivered us to others. They were all convinced that we came from Heaven. (Anything that is new to them or beyond their comprehension is explained as coming from Heaven.) We Christians traveled all day without food, eating only at night—and then so little as to astonish our escort. We never felt tired, being so inured to hardship, which increased our enormous influence over them. To maintain this authority the better, we seldom talked with them directly, but made the Negro our intermediary. He was constantly in conversation, finding out about routes, towns, and other matters we wished to know.

We passed from one strange tongue to another, but God our Lord always enabled each new people to understand us and we them. You would have thought, from the questions and answers in signs, that they spoke our language and we theirs. We did know six Indian languages, but could not always avail ourselves of them; there are a thousand dialectical differences.

Through all these nations, the people who were at war quickly made up so they could come meet us with everything they possessed. Thus we left all the land in peace. And we taught all the people by signs, which they understood, that in Heaven was a Man we called God, who had created the heavens and the earth; that all good came from Him and that we worshipped and obeyed Him and called him our Lord; and that if they would do the same, all would be well with them. They apprehended so readily that, if we had had enough command of their language to make ourselves perfectly understood, we would have left them all Christians.

We told them what we could and, from then on, at sunrise, they would raise their arms to the sky with a glad cry, then run their hands down the length of their bodies. They repeated this ritual at sunset.

They are a substantial people with a capacity for unlimited development.

CHAPTER 49:
The Town of Hearts

IN THE TOWN where the emeralds were presented us, the [Pima] people gave Dorantes over 600 opened deer hearts, which they always kept in great supply for food. So we called this place the Town of Hearts (*Pueblo de los Corazones*). [It stood at or near Ures, on the Río Sonora.] It is the gateway to many provinces on the South Sea, and whoever seeks them without entering here will surely be lost.

The timid, surly Indians of the coast grow no corn; they eat powdered rushes, straw, and fish, which they catch from rafts, having no canoes. The women cover themselves somewhat, with grass and straw.

We think that near the coast, along the line of those permanent towns we came through, must be more than a thousand leagues of settled, productive land, where three crops a year of corn and beans are sown.

Deer in that belt are of three kinds, one of which [the "black tail"] are as big as yearling steers in Castile.

The [Pima and Ópata] houses are of the kind called *bahíos* [or *buhíos*] in the West Indies.

These people get poison from a certain tree [called *mago* in Ópata] which is about the size of our apple trees. All they have to do is pick the fruit and wet the arrow with it or, if there be no fruit, break a twig and the milk will do as well. The tree is so deadly that, if deer or other animals drink where its bruised leaves have been steeped, they will burst.

We stayed in the Town of Hearts three days.

CHAPTER 50:
The Buckle and the Horseshoe Nail

A FEW DAYS farther on [thirty leagues, according to the *Joint Report*] we came to another town [Soyopa] where rain was falling so heavily that we could not cross the swollen [Yaqui] river and had to wait fifteen days. [The *Joint Report* says Christmas came while they waited; all other evidence points to its being late January (1536), but the Spaniards may well have been about a month off in their reckoning by now.]

In this time [which we learn later from Cabeza de Vaca and also from the *Joint Report* was not during the fifteen-day wait but at the next stop twelve leagues on, which would have been Ónovas] Castillo happened to see an Indian wearing around his neck a little sword-belt buckle with a horseshoe nail stitched to it.

He took the amulet, and we asked the Indian what it was. He said it came from Heaven. But who had brought it? He and the Indians with him said that some bearded men like us had come to that river from Heaven, with horses, lances, and swords, and had lanced two natives.

Casually we inquired what had become of those men. They had gone to sea, said the Indians. They had put their lances into the water, got into the water themselves, and finally were seen moving on top of the water into the sunset.

We gave many thanks to God our Lord. Having almost despaired of finding Christians again, we could hardly restrain our excitement. Yet we anxiously suspected that these men were explorers who had merely made a flying visit on their voyage of discovery. But having at last some exact information to go on, we quickened our pace and, as we went, heard more and more of Christians. We told

122

the natives we were going after those men to order them to stop killing, enslaving, and dispossessing the Indians; which made our friends very glad.

We hastened through a vast territory, which we found vacant, the inhabitants having fled to the mountains in fear of Christians. With heavy hearts we looked out over the lavishly watered, fertile, and beautiful land, now abandoned and burned and the people thin and weak, scattering or hiding in fright. Not having planted, they were reduced to eating roots and bark; and we shared their famine the whole way. Those who did receive us could provide hardly anything. They themselves looked as if they would willingly die. They brought us blankets they had concealed from the other Christians and told us how the latter had come through razing the towns and carrying off half the men and all the women and boys; those who had escaped were wandering about as fugitives. We found the survivors too alarmed to stay anywhere very long, unable or unwilling to till, preferring death to a repetition of their recent horror. While they seemed delighted with our company, we grew apprehensive that the Indians resisting farther on at the frontier would avenge themselves on us.

When we got there, however, they received us with the same awe and respect the others had—even more, which amazed us. Clearly, to bring all these people to Christianity and subjection to Your Imperial Majesty, they must be won by kindness, the only certain way.

They took us to a village on the crest of a range of mountains [probably the mountains northeast of San José de Delicias—Hallenbeck]; it was a difficult ascent. The many people who had taken refuge there from the Christians received us well, giving us all they had: over 2,000 backloads of corn, which we distributed to the distressed, pathetic beings who had guided us to that place.

Next day, we despatched four heralds through the country, according to our custom, to call together all the rest of the Indians at a town three *jornadas* distant. We set out, ourselves, the day after that, with all who had congregated on the montain top.

All along the way we could see the tracks of the Christians and traces of their camps. We met our messengers at noon. They had been unable to contact any Indians, who roved the woods out of sight, eluding the Christians. The night before, our heralds had spied on the Christians from behind trees and seen them marching many Indians in chains.

This intelligence terrified our escort, some of whom ran to spread the news that the Christians were coming, and many more would have followed if we had not managed to forbid them and to palliate their fright. We had with us [Pima] Indians from [the Town of Hearts] a hundred leagues back whom we could not at this time discharge with the recompense due them.

For further reassurance to our escort, we held up where we were for the night. The following day we slept on the trail at the end of the *jornada*. The day after that, our heralds guided us to the place they had watched the Christians. We got there that afternoon and saw at once they had told the truth. We noted by the stakes the horses had been tied to that the men were mounted.

From this point, on the Río Pertután [Petatlán, later called the Sinaloa] back to the point where we first heard of the Christians, on the [Yaqui] river which Diego de Guzmán discovered [in 1531], may be as far as eighty leagues [one hundred, according to the *Joint Report*]. From there back to the village where the rains overtook us is another twelve leagues, and this latter place is twelve leagues [actually about forty-five in a straight line] from the South Sea [the Gulf of California].

Throughout this region, wherever we encountered mountains, we saw undeniable indications of gold, antimony, iron, copper, and other metals.

Where the permanent habitations are, the climate is so hot that the weather is quite warm even in January. South from them, the country is mostly uninhabited and barren all the way across to the North Sea [the Gulf of Mexico]. Through that barren country we suffered nearly unendurable hunger. The [Jumano] Indians who roam this region as home are mean beyond belief. Both they and the sedentary Indians, by the way, regard gold and silver with indifference, seeing no use for either.

CHAPTER 51:
The First Confrontation

WHEN WE SAW for certain that we were drawing near the Christians, we gave thanks to God our Lord for choosing to bring us out of such a melancholy and wretched captivity. The joy we felt can only be conjectured in terms of the time, the suffering, and the peril we had endured in that land.

The evening of the day we reached the recent campsite, I tried hard to get Castillo or Dorantes to hurry on three days, unencumbered, after the Christians who were now circling back into the area we had assured protection. They both reacted negatively, excusing themselves for weariness, though younger and more athletic than I; but they being unwilling, I took the Negro and eleven Indians next morning to track the Christians. We went ten leagues, past three villages where they had slept.

The day after that, I overtook four of them [twenty, according to the *Joint Report*] on their horses. They were dumbfounded at the sight of me, strangely undressed and in company with Indians. They just stood staring for a long time, not thinking to hail me or come closer to ask questions.

"Take me to your captain," I at last requested; and we went together half a league to a place [near Ocoroni on the Sinaloa] where we found their captain, Diego de Alcaraz [whom we know from events of the next few days and from the later Coronado expedition as a weak and vicious man].

When we had talked awhile, he confessed to me that he ·was completely undone, having been unable to catch any Indians in a long time; he did not know which way to turn; his men were getting too hungry and exhausted. I told him of Castillo and Dorantes ten leagues away with an escorting multitude. He immediately despatched three of his horsemen to them, along with fifty of his Indian allies. The Negro went, too, as a guide; I stayed behind.

I asked the Christians to furnish mè a certificate of the year, month, and day I arrived here, and the manner of my coming; which they did [but Cabeza de Vaca withholds from us what the date was that they certified; the month would have been March and the year 1536.] From this river [the Sinaloa] to the Christian town, Sant Miguel [the same as Culiacán] within the government of the recently created province of New Galicia, is a distance of thirty leagues.

[Culiacán was then the northernmost Spanish settlement in Mexico. Sauer traces Cabeza de Vaca's route from Ónovas to there via the later-founded towns of Nuri, Concorit, Álamos, El Fuerte, Sinaloa, Comanito, and Pericos. Cabeza de Vaca calls Culiacán both by this original Indian name of the village—which in time officially prevailed— and by its Spanish name. In the 1542 edition he also makes a confusing reference to *Auhacán* which is omitted in the 1555 edition. This reference contains an out-of-place notation of leaving for Culiacán which is restored to its proper place below.]

CHAPTER 52:
The Falling-Out with Our Countrymen

AFTER FIVE DAYS, Andrés Dorantes and Alonso del Castillo arrived with those who had gone for them; and they brought more than 600 natives of the vicinity whom the Indians who had been escorting us drew out of the woods and took to the mounted Christians, who thereupon dismissed their own escort.

When they arrived, Alcaraz begged us to order the villagers of this river out of the woods in the same way to get us food. It would be unnecessary to command them to bring food, if they came at all; for the Indians were always diligent to bring us all they could.

We sent our heralds to call them, and presently there came 600 Indians with all the corn they possessed. They brought it in clay-sealed earthen pots which had been buried. They also brought whatever else they had; but we wished only a meal, so gave the rest to the Christians to divide among themselves.

After this we had a hot argument with them, for they meant to make slaves of the Indians in our train. We got so angry that we went off forgetting the many Turkish-shaped bows, the many pouches, and the five emerald arrowheads, etc., which we thus lost. And to think we had given these Christians a supply of cowhides and other things that our retainers had carried a long distance!

It proved difficult to persuade our escorting Indians to go back to their homes, to feel apprehensive no longer, and to plant their corn. [February being the usual planting time in those parts, there would be a sense of urgency to plant before the crop should be entirely missed.] But they did not want to do anything until they had first delivered us into the hands of other Indians, as custom bound

127

them. They feared they would die if they returned without fulfiling this obligation whereas, with us, they said they feared neither Christians nor lances.

This sentiment roused our countrymen's jealousy. Alcaraz bade his interpreter tell the Indians that we were members of his race who had been long lost; that his group were the lords of the land who must be obeyed and served, while we were inconsequential. The Indians paid no attention to this. Conferring among themselves, they replied that the Christians lied: We had come from the sunrise, they from the sunset; we healed the sick, they killed the sound; we came naked and barefoot, they clothed, horsed, and lanced; we coveted nothing but gave whatever we were given, while they robbed whomever they found and bestowed nothing on anyone.

They spoke thus through the Spaniards' interpreter and, at the same time, to the Indians of other dialects through one of our interpreters. Those who speak the tongue of our interpreter we give the blanket term *Primahaitu,* which is like saying "Biscayans." [Frederick Hodge points out that if Cabeza de Vaca meant *Pimahaitu,* the word meant, literally, "Nothing," since *Pima* means "no" and *haitu* "thing"; the Pimas did not call themselves Pimas but *O-otam*: "people." Their way of saying "no" must have given them the name others knew them by. The analogy to Biscayans evidently only shows how the word might be used in a sentence.] We found this language, and no other, in use for more than 400 leagues. [From the Town of Hearts to Culiacán the Indians along Cabeza de Vaca's way were of the Pima family.]

To the last I could not convince the Indians that we were of the same people as the Christian slavers. Only with the greatest effort were we able to induce them to go back home. We ordered them to fear no more, reestablish their towns, and farm.

Already the countryside had grown rank from neglect. This is, no doubt, the most prolific land in all these Indies. It produces three crops a year; the trees bear a great variety of fruit; and beautiful rivers and brimming springs abound throughout. There are gold- and silver-bearing ores. The people are well disposed, serving such Christians as are their friends with great good will. They are comely, much more so than the Mexicans ["Mexicans" evidently meaning any Indians south of the Pima family]. This land, in short, lacks nothing to be regarded as blest.

When the Indians took their leave of us they said they would do as we commanded and rebuild their towns, if the Christians let them. And I solemnly swear that if they have not done so it is the fault of the Christians.

[The Pimas who had been escorting Cabeza de Vaca and his companions colonized a community at Bamoa, just south of the town of Sinaloa.]

After we had dismissed the Indians in peace and thanked them for their toil in our behalf, the Christians subtly sent us on our way [under arrest] in the charge of an *alcalde* named Cebreros, attended by two horsemen [and a number of Indian allies]. They took us through forests and wastes so we would not communicate with the natives and would neither see nor learn of their crafty scheme afoot. Thus we often misjudge the motives of men; we thought we had effected the Indians' liberty, when the Christians were but poising to pounce.

For two days we wandered lost in the woods without water or trail. Seven of our accompanying Indians died of thirst, and the rest of us got to the brink. Even many of the Indians friendly to the Christians could not manage to reach the place where we finally found water the second night, until noon the third day. We traveled about twenty-five leagues, and came to a village of pacified Indians [at or just below Pericos]. The *alcalde* left us here and went on another three leagues [eight—*Joint Report*] to Culiacán, where resided Melchoir Díaz, *alcalde mayor* and captain of the province.

CHAPTER 53:
The Parley at Culiacán

THE ALCALDE MAYOR happened to know of the Narváez expedition and, hearing now of our return from it, rushed that very night to where we were, and wept with us amid praises to God our Lord.

He provided for us handsomely. In behalf of the governor, Nuño de Guzmán, and himself he put at our disposal everything he had and any service in his power. He greatly regretted our having been seized [arrested] and the general injustice Alcaraz and others had meted us. We felt certain that, had Díaz been there, what the Indians suffered would never have occurred.

Next morning—1 April 1536—after baptizing the children, we set out with Díaz for Culiacán, where the *Alcalde Mayor* prevailed on us to tarry; for, he said, we could do an eminent service to Your Majesty: restore the deserted, wasted, untilled land by sending to and commanding the Indians in the name of God and King to return to their valleys and tend the soil.

This struck us as doubtful of success. We had brought with us neither a servant native nor any of those who had escorted us according to custom who were versed in these procedures. But at last we decided to try it with two Indians from that sorrowful region, who had been captives of the Christians when we first overtook the latter. They had seen the multitude who escorted us and learned from them the great authority we exercised all through their homeland, the wonders we had worked, the sick we had cured, etc. We ordered that they, together with some Indians of Culiacán, go forth and summon the offended natives of the mountains and the Río Petachán [Sinaloa], where we had come upon the Christians, and tell them to come to us for we wanted to speak to them. For our messengers' protection, and as proof that they acted on our authority, we gave them one of the gourds we were used to carrying as our principal symbol of rank.

This delegation was gone seven days. They came back with three *caciques* of the rebel refugees on the ridges, attended by fifteen men. The *caciques* presented us beads, turquoises, and feathers. Our messengers said they had not found the river people where we had been; the Christians had obliged them to scatter to the mountains.

Melchior Díaz bade the interpreter tell the natives that we had come in the name of God in Heaven; that we had journeyed over the world for many years enjoining all the people we met to believe in God and serve Him; for He was master of all things on earth, rewarding the good and punishing the bad in perpetual fire; that when the good die He takes them to Heaven where none die or feel cold, hunger, thirst, or the least inconvenience, but enjoy the greatest conceivable felicity; that those who refuse to believe in Him or obey His commands He casts under the earth to the company of demons, in a great fire that never goes out, in unceasing torment; that if they would like to be Christians and serve God as we required, the Christians would accept them as brothers and treat them kindly—we would command them to give no offense and take no territory from them but be their true friends. If the Indians chose otherwise, the Christians would treat them hard and carry them away to strange lands as slaves.

The *caciques* answered through the interpreter that they would be faithful Christians and serve God. Asked whom they sacrificed to [Cabeza de Vaca shortly says he found no sacrificing among any Indians], worshiped, and entreated for rain and health, they replied: a man in Heaven. We asked his name. Aguar. They said they believed he created the whole world and everything in it. How did they know this? Their fathers and grandfathers had told them; it had been passed down from a distant time; the old men knew that Aguar sent rain and all good things.

We told them we called this deity they spoke of, *Dios,* and if they would call Him this and worship Him as we specified, it would go well with them. They replied they understood well and would do as we said. We ordered them to come down from the mountains fearlessly and peacefully, reinhabit the country and rebuild their houses and, among the latter, they should build one for God with a cross placed over the door like the one we had in the room and that, when Christians came among them, they should go to greet them with crosses in their hands instead of bows or other weapons, take them to their houses and feed them, and the Christians would not harm them but be friends. The Indians told us they would comply.

The Captain [Díaz] concluded with a presentation of shawls and a repast, and they went back, taking the two captives who had served as emissaries. This parley took place before a notary in the presence of many witnesses.

CHAPTER 54:
The Great Transformation

As soon as these Indians got home, all the inhabitants of that province who were friendly to the Christians and had heard of us, came to visit, bearing beads and feathers. We commanded them to build churches with crosses; up to that time none had been erected. We also bade them bring their principal men to be baptized.

Then the Captain made a solemn covenant with God not to invade or consent to invasion, or enslave any of that region we had guaranteed safety; to enforce and defend this sacred contract until Your Majesty and Governor Nuño de Guzmán, or the Viceroy in your name, should direct further as to the service of God and Your Highness.

Indians came to us shortly with tidings that many people

had descended from the mountains and were living again in the valleys; that they had erected churches with crosses, and were doing everything we required. Each day we heard further to the same effect.

Fifteen days after our taking up residence in this town, Alcaraz got back with his cohorts [possibily in response to peremptory orders sent out by Díaz]. They reported to the Captain the way the Indians had come down and repopulated the plain; how they would issue from their formerly deserted villages carrying crosses, take the visitors to their houses and give of what they had. The Christians even slept among these hosts overnight! They could not comprehend such a novelty. Since the natives said their safety had been officially assured, the Christians decided to depart quietly.

We are thankful to our merciful God that it should be in the days of Your Majesty's dominion that these nations might all come voluntarily to Him who created and redeemed us. We are convinced that Your Majesty is destined to do this much and that it is entirely within reason to accomplish. For in the 2,000 leagues we sojourned by land and sea, including ten months' ceaseless travel after escaping captivity, we found no sacrifices and no idolatry.

In that period, we crossed from sea to sea. The data we took great pains to collect indicate that the width of the continent, at its widest, may be 200 leagues [which would be an excellent estimate measuring at the latitude of Culiacán]; and that pearls and great riches are to be found on the coast of the South Sea, near which the best and most opulent of all nations flourishes.

CHAPTER 55:
Arrival in Mexico City

WE STAYED IN Sant Miguel until May 15, the reason being that the devastated and enemy-ridden hundred leagues between there and Compostella, where Governor Nuño de Guzmán resided, required a convoy, which took time to arrange. Twenty mounted men escorted us forty leagues, and then six Christians, with five hundred slaves, escorted us the rest of the way. [A little over one hundred fifty miles on the road to Compostella, at the seaside town · of Mazatlán, Cabeza de Vaca made his closest approach to the Pacific, which, however, could be sighted from the road sometime earlier.]

At Compostella the Governor received us graciously and outfitted us from his wardrobe. I could not stand to wear any clothes for some time, or to sleep anywhere but on the bare floor.

[Cabeza de Vaca does not mention quailing in the presence of five hundred Indian slaves the greater part of the trip from Culiacán, or that his gracious host was the prime mover of the slave raids in the Pima country. Guzmán was an extremely able man and, on occasion, charming, but also exceedingly cruel and predatory. Had the Narváez expeditionaries made it to Pánuco as they intended, they would have been received by Guzmán, who was then governor at that northernmost Spanish outpost. In the years Cabeza de Vaca ranged eastern Texas as a merchant, Guzmán founded Culiacán, the northernmost Spanish outpost in western Mexico (farther north than Pánuco). He also founded Compostella and Guadalajara, naming the latter after his own home town in Spain. He outraged the Spanish as well as the Indian population wherever he

134

operated and had made mortal enemies of the other three most powerful men in New Spain: the Viceroy, Cortés, and the Archbishop. It was the licentiate Diego Pérez de la Torre, however, who as special investigator was closing in on Guzmán at the time Cabeza de Vaca was his guest and who had the Governor in jail within eight months.]

After ten or twelve days, we left for Mexico City [now mounted, by Guzmán's generosity], and all the way enjoyed the hospitality of Christians, numbers of whom came out on the road to see us, giving thanks to God for preserving us through so many calamities. [Their route lay along the already-established highway, via Guadalajara —a total distance from Culiacán to Mexico City of slightly over 900 miles.]

We rode into Mexico City on Sunday [July 24], the day before the vespers of Santiago [Saint James] and were royally and joyously received by the Viceroy [the great first one, Antonio de Mendoza] and the Marqués del Valle [the great *conquistador*, Cortés], who gave us clothes and offered whatever else they had.

The day of Santiago was celebrated with a *fiesta* and a bullfight.

CHAPTER 56:
My Voyage Home

AFTER TWO MONTHS' rest in Mexico City, I wanted to get back to these kingdoms but, when about to embark [at Veracruz] in October, a storm blew up which capsized the ship, and she was lost. So I decided to stay on for the winter, a boisterous season in those parts for navigation.

Dorantes and I left Mexico City during Lent [1537] to catch an early spring sailing from Veracruz and had to wait till Palm Sunday for a wind. We went aboard Palm Sunday and then had to wait another fifteen days for the wind to resume. The ship leaked so badly that I transferred to one of two other vessels ready to depart, but Dorantes remained on the leaky one.

At last, on April 10, the three ships cleared port and sailed 150 leagues. Two of them were leaking alarmingly; one night, they ceased to keep company with the ship I rode. We afterwards learned that their pilots and skippers dared not go farther and put back into Veracruz without warning us. When my ship pulled into the Harbor at Havana on May 4, we waited for the other ships until June 2, when we went on in dread of falling in with French pirates who had taken three Spanish vessels a few days before. What took us, instead, was a violent storm at the island of Bermuda. Those who pass there from time to time say such storms are fairly regular. We thought ourselves lost one whole night when, to our relief, the storm subsided with morning, and we continued our course.

[The stopover at Santo Domingo is not mentioned. Obviously, the *Joint Report,* which Cabeza de Vaca delivered to the Audiencia there had been composed in Mexico City—possibly a duplicate of the report to the Viceroy that has been lost.]

In twenty-nine days out of Havana we had sailed 1,100 leagues, supposedly the distance to the Azores and, sure enough, next morning we passed the island of Corvo, but, as we did, fell in with a French ship. She took up the chase at noon, bringing along a Portuguese caravel captured earlier. That evening we made out nine more sail, but they were so far away we could not tell whether they were Portuguese or French.

After nightfall the Frenchmen got within lombard shot of us, and we stole from our course in the dark, hoping to evade him. Three or four times we did this. He got near enough to us once to see us, and fired. He could have taken us, either then or at his leisure next morning. I will never forget my gratitude to the Almighty when, with the sunrise, we recognized the nine sail closing in to be of the fleet of Portugal. I gave thanks to our Lord for His shielding hand against the perils of land and sea alike.

As soon as the Frenchman identified the nine sail, he let go the caravel which carried a cargo of Negroes, to make us think the caravel was Portuguese so we might wait for her. On casting her off, the Frenchman told her pilot and skipper that we were French and under his convoy. Suddenly sixty oars sprouted from the Frenchman and he moved out with incredible speed. The caravel went to the galleon and informed the commander that both we and the racing ship were French. The fleet therefore thought we might be bearing down upon them as we drew nigh, and bore up for us in battle formation. When we had converged close enough, we hailed them; and the discovery that we were friends was also the discovery that they had been duped into letting the pirate get away. Four caravels were sent in pursuit.

When the galleon came alongside, the commander, Diego de Silveira, called out to our captain: "Whence come ye, and what may be your merchandise?"

"From New Spain, laden with silver and gold."

"How much?"

"Three thousand *castellanos*."

"Ye do truly come passing rich, and such a sorry ship —sorrier artillery. Chee! That French son of a bitch missed a luscious morsel! Now mind that ye stick to my rear, that I may, with God's help, get you to Spain."

The caravels did not keep up their pursuit for long and came back. The Frenchman was too fast for them but, also, they hated to leave the fleet, which was guarding three spice-laden ships. So we made the island of Terceira and languished there fifteen days imbibing refreshment while awaiting the arrival of another Portuguese merchantman coming with a cargo from India to join the three spice ships and their convoy.

Time ran out and it did not show, so we left with the fleet and anchored in the port of Lisbon on August 9, on the eve of the day of our master Sant Laurencio, 1537.

CHAPTER 57:
What Became of the Others
Who Went to the Indies

I NEED TO CLEAR UP what happened to the ships of the
Narváez expedition and the people who remained in them.
The reason I have not touched on this before now is that
we were uninformed until we reached New Spain, where
we found many of the individuals who had been aboard;
I found more here in Castile. From all these, everything
to the last detail finally came out.

At the time we split from the ships, one of them had
already been lost in the breakers and the other three faced
a dangerous prospect, with low stores and nearly a hundred souls on board, ten of them married women.

. One of these women had prophesied to the Governor
many things that later actually befell him. She warned him
before he plunged inland not to go; that he nor anyone
with him could ever escape; though should one get back,
the Almighty must work great wonders for him. She, however, believed few or none would be seen again. The Governor said that, after all, he and his men were going to fight
and conquer wholly unknown nations, and of course he
knew that this would cost many slain; but the survivors
would indeed be fortunate from what he understood of
the riches of that land. Yet he begged her to tell him where
she had got her notions of what was going to happen that
was past as well as these things still to come, and she replied that they had been told her in Castile by a Moorish
woman of Hornachos. She had said the same thing to us
even before we left Spain, and many things happened on
the passage in the way she foretold.

On making Caravallo, a native of Cuenca de Huete,

lieutenant and commander of the vessels and the people on them, the Governor left orders for going immediately aboard and taking the direct course to Pánuco, closely examining along shore for the harbor and, when finding it, holding up inside it until our arrival; and then the Governor departed. The people of the ships state that, when they had got back on board, they distinctly heard that woman say to the other women that their husbands were the same as dead and that they might as well be looking after whom they would marry next; she was going to. And she did presently "marry." So did the other wives "marry" with men who remained in the ships.

When we were gone, the vessels made sail and took their course as instructed but, missing the harbor, returned. Five leagues below the place we debarked, they came upon the port where we had found crates with corpses. Meanwhile, the other ship and the brigantine arrived from Cuba and they altogether looked for us for nearly a year and, finally giving us up, went on to New Spain. [Hallenbeck conjectures that the barges and these ships must have passed within a short distance of each other in opposite directions, probably at night.]

The harbor of which I speak [Tampa Bay] is the best in the world. It has six fathoms of water at its entrance and five near shore. It stretches inland seven or eight leagues. Its bottom is fine white sand; no sea breaks upon it or wild storm; and it can contain countless vessels. Fish is plentiful. It is but a hundred leagues from Havana, a town of Christians in Cuba, with which it bears north and south. Vessels go from the one harbor to the other in a round trip of only a few days because, with the constant northeast wind, they sail either way with it on the quarter.

And now it may be well to state fully who the persons are whom our Lord pleased to release from these troubles, and what parts of these kingdoms they hail from:

1. Alonso del Castillo Maldonado, native of Salamanca, son of Doctor Castillo and Doña Aldonza Maldonado.

2. Andrés Dorantes, son of Pablo Dorántes, native of Béjar and citizen of Gibraleon.

Afterword

[CASTILLO DID NOT SAIL to Spain with Cabeza de Vaca but did sail at some other time, only to return to Mexico, where he married a well-to-do widow and was granted half the rents of the Indian town of Tehuacán. As a citizen of Mexico City, he slips quietly from history's sight.

When Dorantes's unseaworthy ship returned to Mexico, the Viceroy Mendoza offered him a commission to explore to the north. He did serve Mendoza in the conquest of Jalisco but, according to the chronicler of De Soto's expedition, Dorantes awaited a joint command with Cabeza de Vaca. He married a land-rich widow, Doña María de la Torre, by whom he had a large family, including three sons who rose to prominence in the enjoyment of their inherited wealth. He had first settled with Mendoza by selling him Estevánico.

This lusty Arab from the Atlantic shore of Morocco (by the way, called "brown" by Diego de Guzmán, who saw him in Sinaloa) became, then, the guide for Fray Marcos of Nice, Father Provincial of the Franciscans of New Spain, who commanded an expedition to the pueblo country as a forerunner of Coronado. Estevánico collected an escort of Indians in the old manner as he strode north, flaunting his sacred gourd rattle. But he introduced a new twist: He required the villages along his way to give him turquoises and beautiful women. In his confidence and his eagerness to be the sole discoverer of the pueblos, he had got eighty leagues ahead of Fray Marcos when he reached Háwikuh, the southernmost of the seven pueblos, about fifteen miles southwest of Zuñi, New Mexico. The shrewd elders of Háwikuh, however, concluded that he must be a spy preceding would-be conquerors; they suspected his statement that he came from a country where people are white, when he was so dark; and they resented his demand for turquoises and women. They put him to death.

Cabeza de Vaca did not know the fate of Juan Ortiz,

141

who came of a noble family of Seville and who happened
to be among the twenty or thirty sailors Narváez sent back
to Cuba in a pinnace for emergency provisions. Señora
Narváez, in Cuba, saw to the loading and hastened the
pinnace back to Sarasota Bay. There Ortiz and a friend,
over the protests of their fellows, went ashore to pick up
what appeared to be a letter from the Governor in a forked
stick. Indians seized the two and killed the friend when he
offered resistance. They prepared an elaborate execution
for Ortiz, but a girl of the tribe effectively interceded
(about eighty years before Captain John Smith near
Jamestown). Set to guarding dead bodies from wolves at
night, Ortiz gained esteem by a lucky dart-throw which
felled a wolf that was carrying off the corpse of a child of
a leading tribesman. He came close to execution again
anyway, sometime later; the girl who had first saved his
life saved it again with a timely warning. He fled south to
a rival *cacique,* Mocozo; De Soto's lieutenant (and a kins-
man of Cabeza de Vaca), Baltasar de Gallegos, found him
in an open field near Charlotte Harbor with ten or twelve
Indians, his arms tattooed just like theirs. When the cavalry
detail charged, Ortiz cried out that he was a Christian and
these Indians had kept him alive. The cavalrymen de-
lightedly carried them to De Soto behind their saddles.
Ortiz died while the expedition wintered at Autiamque,
thirty miles south of Fort Smith, Arkansas, sometime before 6 March 1542, much lamented by De Soto, who
thereby lost his only interpreter.

Vasco Porcallo de Figueroa, the prominent gentleman
of Trinidad, Cuba, who, we have seen, lost a brother on the
Narváez expedition (he should not be confused with
Figueroa, the excellent swimmer from Toledo), was made
captain-general by De Soto when De Soto "busted" the
philanderer who had held that office. The new appointment
proved a boon to the commissary, for Porcallo donated a
great many hogs and loads of cassava bread. He, however,
fell out with De Soto on the west coast of Florida; for all
he was interested in was slaves for his plantation and
mines, and the dense forests and extensive bogs prevented

the seizures he had hoped to make. He headed back to his Cuban holdings in 1539.

The good *alcalde mayor,* Captain Melchoir Díaz, accepted a command under Coronado in 1540. Early that fall, he and a detachment of his, out of Sonora, crossed the lower Colorado on rafts, and, somewhere on the west coast of the Gulf of California one day, a soldier's greyhound started chasing some of the sheep of the train. The captain hurled a lance at the dog from a running horse at high speed; the lance stuck solidly in the ground; the horse overran it, and it punctured Díaz's bladder. On the twentieth day that his men carried him while retreating through hostile territory he died.

The official communiqué of his death came from none other than the Guzmán henchman, Diego de Alcaraz, whom Cabeza de Vaca met on the Sinaloa and fell out with so heatedly that he was arrested. Díaz had left Alcaraz in command at Sonora, where he continued in his callous ways with impunity. Late in 1541, however, he lay sick at Suya, on the San Pedro near the Arizona border, his riffraff followers having largely deserted him to fall back on Culiacán, when stealthy Indians, apparently Sobaipuri, surprised the village near dawn. They mortally wounded Alcaraz as a few aides helped him away.

As to Nuño de Guzmán, that high-riding host who furnished clothes and horses for Cabeza de Vaca and his companions, the implacable Pérez de la Torre toppled him from his Compostella perch on 19 January 1537. The ex-Governor's appeal from jail in Mexico City failed and, remitted dispossessed to Spain in July 1538, he continued in detention, first at Torrejón de Velasco and later at Valladolid, until his death in 1550.]

Epilogue

"How shall a man endure the will of God and the days of the silence?" asks the narrator of Archibald MacLeish's poem *Conquistador*. This is the kind of riddle that Alvar Nuñez Cabeza de Vaca might have posed himself during the eight years he roamed the coastal marshes and mountains and deserts of what is now the American Southwest. Like the great conquerors he marched by "a king's name," discovered a "famous country," and suffered "unknown hardships." But the only enemies he fought and subdued were his own body and will. Cabeza de Vaca's conquest lay in the realm of the spirit rather than that of territory and treasure.

The historical significance of Cabeza de Vaca's wanderings with three companions over six thousand miles and eight years cannot be doubted. The Spaniards' adventures in the uncharted lands to the north ignited considerable greed and ambition when the wanderers appeared in Mexico City in 1536. The tales the travelers brought back with them—tales in which they insisted they had seen evidence along their route of "gold, antimony, iron, copper, and other metals" (p. 124)—were listened to with growing excitement. These stories, no doubt greatly exaggerated as they passed from person to person, soon revived rumors of the Seven Cities of Cíbola and eventually prompted the Coronado expedition, as the Preface to this book points out. The adventures of Cabeza de Vaca and his companions, then, were the first link in a chain of events that resulted in the Spanish colonization of the Southwest.

But Cabeza de Vaca's more lasting significance has been literary and cultural, not historical. The report he published in 1542 under the title *La Relación* has fascinated and puzzled readers for centuries. A backward glance at that work reveals that Cabeza de Vaca was not only a physical trailblazer; he was also a literary pioneer, and he deserves the distinction of being called the Southwest's first writer. His narrative turned out to be a prototype of much American writing to come; it is, without question, the most remarkable product of the Spaniard's eight-year odyssey.

La Relación possesses many of the attributes of a good novel—especially its subtle preséntation of character and its dramatic tension, which is a natural outgrowth of the true storyline. Its scope, as befits its function as a "report," is broad enough to include much information about the country through which the wanderers passed—the variety of its climate, its flora and fauna, the customs of its natives. Cabeza de Vaca was apparently an interested observer, even under the most extreme conditions, and his descriptions of man and nature in the pre-European Southwest are helpful to historians, anthropologists, and other present-day scholars. The facet of the narrative that has intrigued readers down through the centuries, however, is less easily defined. *La Relación's* laconic style often conceals more than it reveals, but it is the recurring understatements that prove most suggestive in their implications. I, want to discuss briefly a few of those implications.

Though Cabeza de Vaca was by birth a European, his narra-tive was shaped by the exigencies of a new and strange environ-ment, and it seems to me a peculiarly American document. On of its underlying themes, for example, is the physica' emotional struggle for an accommodation between r. conflict that has never been very far removed from the Am. consciousness and one that has always been a factor in the wᵤrks of our best and most vital writers; further, the narrative leans decidedly toward the metaphysical; and finally it is couched in an allegorical framework (for Cabeza de Vaca it was also a structure of reality) that has often been employed by American writers, great and obscure. In these ways *La Relación* points to the forms and thematic concerns of important segments of later American literature.

Cabeza de Vaca's attitude toward Indians—his increasing sympathy and admiration for the native Americans he met along his route—is the crux of the work's racial theme. The history of the Spanish in the New World shows that they, like other colonizing groups, were arrogant and often brutal in their relations with the Indian population. Cabeza de Vaca, when he began his great adventure, must have had in him something of the conquistador's haughty view of the Indian. He was, after all, an aristocrat, and his grandfather, Pedro de Vera, had cruelly suppressed the Canary Islanders and, in so doing, incurred the denunciation of the Church. But after eight years among the native Americans, Cabeza de Vaca's attitude toward them had changed to one of kindness and (within the limits of his time and place) understanding.

Though the modern reader may find a touch of condescension in Cabeza de Vaca's advice to his king concerning the native Americans, it is nonetheless worth quoting: "to bring all these people to Christianity and subjection to Your Imperial Majesty, they must be won by kindness, the only certain way" (p. 123). As he progressed in his journey, the Spaniard became more and more aware that the native Americans, despite their (to him) bizarre customs, were indeed human beings who, like himself, responded to friendliness and charity. Part of this recognition was perhaps the result of his natural compassion for human misery and suffering, which he had an opportunity to observe firsthand as the sick of village after village were brought to him for treatment. But apart from pity, he approved of the Indians of the interior for their admirable physical and mental traits.

It is revealing that the Indians, in reciprocation, came almost to worship the four Spaniards. Cabeza de Vaca comments that, at the end of their journey, Alcarez, the slave-hunter, had told the assembled Indians that the wanderers were Christians like himself and his men; the Indians refused to believe him, for

> we had come from the sunrise, they from the sunset; we
> healed the sick, they killed the sound; we came naked and

barefoot, they clothed, horsed, and lanced; we coveted nothing but gave whatever we were given, while they robbed whomever they found and bestowed nothing on anyone. (p. 128)

This, in succinct contrast, was the difference between men who had learned a great lesson during their eight years of hardship and privation—the lesson of brotherhood and human kinship— and officials fettered by the colonial mentality.

La Relación, then, in its account of racial difference, and of the misunderstandings and conflicts engendered by that difference, anticipates much later American writing. It is a forerunner, in another sense, because of the unmistakable spiritual quality it radiates. It is perhaps a critical commonplace, but an essential one, to insist on a fundamental distinction between European and American letters. In general, European literature, fiction in particular, excells in the recounting of the minutiae of life, in depicting manners, social and political, whereas American books are often concerned with ultimates—with a person's relationships to God, to the universe, and to his own soul. Most works of American literature, says W. H. Auden, "are parables; their settings, even when they pretend to be realistic, symbolic settings for a timeless and unlocated (because internal) psychomachia." Cabeza de Vaca's narrative was ostensibly composed as a chronicle of physical ordeal, but many readers who have searched for its deeper meanings have detected a corresponding odyssey of the spirit, have seen in it a kind of true-life "parable."

The element of spirituality in the work that immediately snares the reader's attention is the Spaniards' activities as faith-healers among the Indians they met along the way. Cabeza de Vaca included in *La Relación* a catalogue of miracles of healing that he and companions supposedly performed. Some commentators have claimed the "miracles" were not genuine; the Indians were lying, the argument runs, when they said they were cured, or perhaps their ailments were psychological in origin and the Spaniards managed to relieve them by means of what we would now call the self-fulfilling prophecy. Others have been more charitable in their interpretations.

One of the most interesting explanations is contained in a curious little book by Haniel Long, called *Interlinear to Cabeza de Vaca* (republished under the less fortunate title *The Power Within Us*). Long's Whitmanesque theory is certainly provocative. It is his belief that Cabeza de Vaca found in the wilderness the secret of tapping that reservoir of power that is in each of us, a power few of us are ever able to exert. By being stripped naked, spiritually as well as physically, the Spaniard was thrust "into a world where nothing, if done for another, seems impossible." He recognized, at the close of his journey, that "the power of maintaining life in others lives within each of us, and from each of us does it recede when unused."

Whether or not the reader accepts Long's latter-day transcendentalism, he must admit the difficulty of explaining the "miracles" in purely rationalistic terms. They seem in any case to have had a profound effect on the one who performed them. Cabeza de Vaca's experiences elevated his spirit to a domain above the physical landscape around him and contributed to the near mysticism—or perhaps it was only a kind of fevered asceticism brought on by hunger and pain—into which he apparently lapsed. The knowledge of human suffering and its psychological, if not physical, alleviation seemed to expand and alter his vision of life; it chastened him, taught him humility, and encouraged his spiritual growth—growth which paralleled with almost calculated artistry his geographic progress.

One of the recurring motifs of American literature is the voyage of exploration, of physical and spiritual discovery, the journey to the interior, in which the dominant figure is man isolated—alone in the wilderness, alone with himself. This thematic and structural device appears with great frequency in our writing. Voyages and journeys of discovery, Harry Levin suggests (in *The Power of Blackness*), "have served as real and imaginary vehicles for our literature from John Smith to Ernest

Hemingway.'' Levin's claim is demonstrably true, but we must look earlier than the English Captain Smith to find the first account of the American journey inward; Cabeza de Vaca's *La Relación* is, in fact, the prototype for such accounts.

La Relación's similarity to the canon of American writing suggests that our literature is what it is because, given the nature of our national experience, it could be nothing else. The exploration and settlement of vast tracts of "empty" land are crucial components of the American's (and especially the Westerner's) heritage, and these historical facts have had to be examined and interpreted in works of a truly national character. A convenient medium for their dramatization, then, has been the journey of discovery. As a literary convention it allows the writer to juxtapose the objective dangers of physical isolation with the subtle and sometimes more demanding trial of spiritual isolation.

The American journey of discovery ends in one of two ways: in hope or in bleak despair. In recent times, as the world has grown progressively darker, it has usually concluded with the latter, with its course leading nowhere. What the modern wanderer normally discovers is a blank, the spiritual equivalent of the nihilistic landscape through which he has trekked. In the case of Cabeza de Vaca, however, rescue seems to have found him a wiser and nobler person than he was when he began. The Spaniard did not rage and storm at fate for casting him ashore among savages and the elements. He accepted the abuse and suffering forced upon him, and as a result he grew and learned. The land fascinated him, and more importantly he came to acknowledge his kinship with the native Americans. It is fitting that he became the first American—his citizenship having been forged in the crucible of pain and privation—to experience and report a sequence of events which, with variations, runs in a continuous stream through our literature.

Three English translations of Cabeza de Vaca's narrative have been published. Thomas Buckingham Smith's, completed in 1851, is available in *Spanish Explorers in the Southern*

United States (1970), edited by Frederick W. Hodge. Fanny Bandelier's was brought out as *The Journey of Alvar Nuñez Cabeza de Vaca* (1905). Cyclone Covey's *Adventures in the Unknown Interior of America,* first published in 1961, is the most recent translation. For the present-day reader it is also the most accessible. Covey's translation is thoughtful and balanced, avoiding an archaic tone as well as twentieth-century colloquialisms. The editor's internal notes are welcome help in orienting the reader to modern placenames and landmarks. As I have tried to show, Cabeza de Vaca's narrative is one of those works essential to a proper understanding of American literature and culture. All students of that literature and culture ought to read and reread it. Its availability in a handsome quality paperback edition should make the task pleasant and easy.

William T. Pilkington
Tarleton State University
Stephenville, Texas

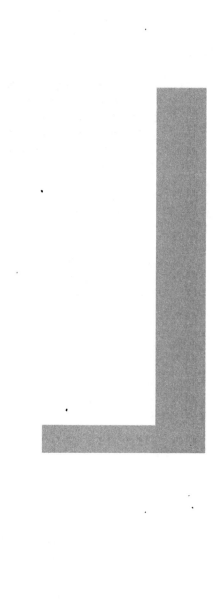

Index

Printed in the USA
CPSIA information can be obtained
at www.ICGtesting.com
LVHW061528160823
755421LV00003B/88